WINCHESTER :

ITS HISTORY, BUILDINGS AND PEOPLE

a. College. shewing Wykeham's original Tower..........1. Kings Gate. with S^t
b. St Stephen's Chapel ....m. Close Gate ....
c. Wolvesey Palace. SE Tower shewing ledges at foot. o. City Wall ....
d........ditto Chapel. on site of present Chapel........ p Close Wall} on eith^r s^tswin
e. Great Keep. shewing columns laid in Wall..........q. South Gate, South
f. Great Hall......g. Gateway towards Town..........r. Prior's House. No
h. St Michael's Church.... j. Susterne Spital........S Monk's Refectory
k. Pilgrims' Hall of Monastery ....t. Cloisters. Cha

KEY TO SMA

Winchester:

Its History,
Buildings and People

Third and
Revised Edition

By the
W. C. A. S.

Winchester: P. & G. Wells Ltd.
Booksellers to Winchester College
—
1933

First Edition 1913
Second Edition (revised)... ... 1921
Third Edition (revised) 1933

PREFACE

For this latest impudence of a School Society no further apology is offered than the book itself. As is indicated by the title, it is the work of the Archaeological Society, and represents substantially the papers read in the Spring of 1913, supplemented by the contributions of some former members. It is designed to give in brief a sketch of the history, buildings, and life of the city. For uniformity's sake each paper consists of three parts answering to those divisions.

For our facts, as being all at secondhand, we claim no merit of originality, and undertake no burden of responsibility. Much that has been called in question by modern critics, we have deliberately stated as fact, preferring to steer clear of controversy. It has rather been our design to present a plain, clear story of the town, and to enable the reader to form in his mind some picture of its past. Living in our quiet humdrum way, it is too seldom that we remember the stirring times our city has witnessed, the great part she has played in the making of England. Each time we step out of our houses we tread on ground that has known the feet of kings and queens, makers of history and writers of noble books, great villains and great saints.

Perhaps, as he meets them in these pages, the reader will now and again pause to call in mind how Alfred, Rufus, Wykeham, and the rest, all in their time, looked out on the same Itchen valley and the same Twyford Downs, and the thought may lend some glamour even to the dry facts of archaeological research.

The contributors' names are as follows :—M. E. Antrobus, F. H. Brabant, G. T. Cartland, A. R. Cross, J. D. Eccles, S. S. G. Leeson, A. G. Macdonnell, H. E. L. Montgomery, E. S. Pearson, and C. F. A. Warner. We also wish to express our debt to Canon Vaughan and N. C. H. Nisbet, Esq., for their kindness in revising the papers.

From a College Street Window.

PREFACE TO SECOND EDITION

THE First Edition of this book being exhausted, it seems high time that another should be issued ; for no rival has appeared to take its place. Since the original work was done in 1913, Mr. A. K. Cook's invaluable commentary on Mathew's poem has appeared, giving us much new information about College. Canon Vaughan has produced his two books on the Cathedral and the Close, Mr. Chitty and others have continued their researches ; nor has the Society itself been idle. It therefore seemed desirable that in the new Edition such fresh matter, as is relevant, should now be added ; and a drastic revision has accordingly been taken in hand. Much of the original text has been re-written, and, as we hope, improved. Footnotes have been added, and the Chapter on College has been entirely transformed by the original author. Most of the revision, and the still more arduous task of re-editing the book, stands to the credit of F. J. Birkbeck (College). C. G. Stevens (College) has re-drawn the plans and pictures ; while other members of the Society have rendered useful aid. Special thanks are due to Mr. Cook, Mr. Hardy, and Mr. Chitty for their kindly help, more particularly in the revision of the chapter upon College.

The other sources of our information, whether literary or otherwise, it would here be superfluous to enumerate, but we trust that, thanks to them and the work of the new editors, the value of this small book will be considerably increased when it appears in its new form. One original defect has at least been remedied ; for there is now an Index.

PREFACE TO THIRD EDITION

THIS Edition has been revised throughout, and in many places re-written. Mr. C. F. C. Hawkes of the British Museum is responsible for the Roman and pre-Roman sections. Mr. C. P. Wright has written a section on the Domestic Architecture of Winchester, and has revised the Appendix on Mediaeval Architecture ; he was also responsible for re-drawing several of the illustrations and plans. M. Maclagan (A) has described the Cathedral in the time of Queen Anne, and its subsequent history has been added by J. Paynter (COLLEGE) and R. L. M. Synge (COLLEGE). The chapter on Winchester College has been extended by Mr. G. H. Blore, and is no longer fifty years out of date. The Chronological Table has also been brought up to date and partly re-written. The editing was begun by M. Maclagan, J. M. Stevens (COLLEGE) and Mr. C. P. Wright, and completed by J. Paynter and R. L. M. Synge. We should like to express our gratitude to Canon Goodman for his help on the early history of the City and Cathedral, and to the Headmaster for his general supervision of the work.

July, 1933.

CONTENTS

LIST OF ILLUSTRATIONS

History of the City
before the Norman Conquest

" YOURS is an ancient city, Mr. Mayor ? " " It
have-a-been, your Majesty, it have-a-been."

The sense of the Mayor's answer to Queen
Elizabeth was better than his grammar. Winchester is so ancient that its first beginnings lie
behind the scope of recorded history. Archaeology
indeed can come forward with its patient interpretation of the history latent in potsherds, coins,
implements, and earthworks, but the tale it has
to tell is at present far from a complete one.
Even in Roman times the written word helps us
but little, and thereafter, when the decline of the
Western Empire brings in our Anglo-Saxon forefathers, the archaeologist and the literary historian
are apt to find themselves at loggerheads. Detailed
criticism of the Anglo-Saxon Chronicle is as
thorny a subject as the Homeric question, and
when our problems are aggravated by the chrono-
logy of Anglo-Saxon ornament and armament,
caution is plainly the better part of wisdom.
Thus justification must be pleaded for its dis-
cernible effects in this initial chapter.

It is clear that Winchester was an important
centre even before the Romans settled here, for
recent excavations on St. Catharine's Hill have
revealed much of the history of the fortified
settlement which crowned it in the pre-Roman
Iron Age.

In the Early Iron Age life was mainly con-
centrated on the open uplands, and forested and

swampy valleys were avoided. But the Belgic invaders of the 1st century B.C. turned to developing the low ground, and it is they who are now credited with founding Winchester.

St. Catharine's Hill is thus, directly or indirectly, the city's predecessor, and it stands looking down on it as do many other Celtic ' hill-forts ' on their daughter towns of Belgic or Roman foundation : Trundle Hill on Chichester, for instance, and Maiden Castle on Dorchester.

Its history is altogether more ancient. Save somewhere about 500 B.C., in the earlier stages of the Iron Age, when Celtic settlers from the Continent were slowly spreading over Britain, one tribe, perhaps, decided to occupy the rounded knob of a hill, which projected from the main ridge of the downs. This place had the double advantage of overlooking the Itchen valley— always a channel of commerce and invasion— and of being well defended by its precipitous contours. At first the settlers had not enough man power to make any artificial defences, but later they threw a ringwork around the brow of the hill, carefully laying it out so that there should be no dead ground. One gap was left in the ramparts ; from this a road ran north-east along the connecting ridge and joined the ancient upland track from Salisbury Plain to Sussex.

The inhabitants then settled down to a peaceful life, having pursuits both pastoral and agricultural, as is indicated by the abundant remains of ox, sheep, pig, horse and dog found in the excavations, and also by the outlines of their fields still visible to the north of Hockley golf course from across the valley. None of their clothing was found, naturally, but spindle whorls and loom weights show that they spun yarn and made cloth.

They made pottery for cooking and storing purposes, but being hand-made much of it was rough, and it was at first only ornamented by applied bands, scratches and fingerprints. Later, in the 3rd and 2nd centuries B.C., the standard improved, and smoother burnished ware was produced, decorated with more regular tooled patterns.

The inhabitants of St. Catharine's Hill used for dwelling and store-places large pits dug in the solid chalk and roofed over with skins or thatch. It seems probable that these pit-dwellings were not the only form of habitation, and that there were also huts on the surface ; the poorer folk were doubtless content with mere shacks and did their cooking in the open.

Just as the entrance was the focus of the camp, so it was its weak point, and in this area can be traced the military history of the camp, throughout its existence. When first the ramparts were erected, the entrance was only defended by guard houses on either side of a wooden gate, which was hinged upon a central post. In a time of security these guard houses fell into disuse and were dismantled. A long and peaceful period passed and then suddenly a war scare came : the ditch was re-cut, the ramparts raised to a height of 25 feet above the ditch and inturned by the entrance, which was additionally masked by a couple of " counterscarp " banks on either side. The guard houses were replaced and half the roadway blocked by a chalk wall and stockade. All these works were carried out with picks of deer horn and shovels made of the shoulder-blades of oxen, and therefore, though small in scale, were vastly laborious and a considerable accomplishment.

The scare passed and the road was once more opened, when suddenly, perhaps about 150 B.C., came the final destruction ; the defences were fired and the entrance blocked with debris, soon to assume its present appearance.

There are few signs of occupation on St. Catharine's Hill after the catastrophe. Across the river, however, the similar but unfortified Celtic settlement at Stanmore certainly lasted till the Roman conquest, as did the more important site on Worthy Down. Here the earlier occupations, corresponding to that of St. Catharine's Hill, were superseded about 50 B.C. by the Belgic invaders from northern Gaul, who were evidently fugitives from Caesar's conquest. Whether it was they who stormed and burnt the defences of St. Catharine's Hill is uncertain : the material found in the excavations did not seem to last as late as 50 B.C., but comparative work elsewhere may one day supply an answer. At any rate, there is no doubt that they were the first regular settlers on the site of Winchester, where their pottery and other relics have been found in low-level digging, and hence it came about that under Roman rule the place became Venta Belgarum, the market-town and capital of the Belgic tribal canton.

Coming of the Belgae

The Roman Conquest

In the conquest on which Claudius embarked in A.D. 43, this part of Britain was reduced by the IInd Legion under Vespasian. The camp at Ashley is apparently a relic of these campaigns, but armed forces can hardly have remained long in the district. Roman Winchester was essentially a centre of peaceful provincial life.

Roman Remains

When a builder digs the foundations of a new house, or the Town Council excavates a drain, Roman remains are often disclosed. In spite of

4

this it is impossible to ascertain the exact position of the Roman walls. The natural supposition is that they lie beneath the foundations of the mediaeval walls. During some excavations in the last century a large mass of masonry, the mortar of which was suspected of being Roman, was in fact dug up under the mediaeval walls. However, notwithstanding the superficial similarity of shape and the remains which have been found, it has been contended that the Roman town may in fact have been somewhat smaller than its mediaeval successor. Whatever may have been the exact area of the Roman settlement, its road system continued to exercise a lasting influence on the history of the town. The Roman roads from Winchester were five in number, and converged on the various gates of the city. From the Northgate emerged two, the one leading to Cirencester (the modern Andover Road) and the other to Silchester (the modern Basingstoke Road) ; from the Westgate ran the road to Old Sarum ; from the Southgate to Clausentum (Bitterne : the modern Southampton Road) ; from the East one led over Dongas to Portus Magnus (Portchester), *via* Owslebury (the modern Portsmouth Road).

Inside the walls there were two main streets See Plan, p. 12 cutting one another in the shape of a cross (now High Street and Southgate Street continued to the north). The latter, running north and south, was kept well up the hill towards the Westgate, in order to avoid the swampy ground near the river. According to their usual custom it is probable that the Romans placed their Law Tribunals in the south-west corner, and their Temples in the south-east corner. This would explain why in later days the Castle stood on the

5

hill, while the Cathedral, which perhaps occupies the site of a Roman Temple, stood down in the swamp.

All manner of Roman relics have been dug up, and there is no space to tell of foundations of houses, or tessellated pavements (one found on the site of the new Cathedral buttresses of 1910 was transferred to the Deanery porch), or coins of many emperors, from Claudius to Honorius at the end of the 4th century. Outside the gates, too, were cemeteries, where cremated burials in urns and later inhumation-graves have often been found.

One or two sidelights on the life of Roman Winchester call for special notice. The first is an altar, the only one found ; it bears an inscription, which reads as follows :—" MATRIB(us) ITAL(i)S GERMANIS GAL(lis) BRIT(annis) (A)NTONIUS (LU)CRETIANUS B(ene)F(iciarius) COS REST(ituit)," which is interpreted to mean that one Antonius Lucretianus, a consular attaché, restored the altar to the Italian, German, and British " Mothers." The *matres* mentioned were three Celtic goddesses, much worshipped in Gaul during the first three centuries A.D., and especially popular with the soldiers. If Lucretianus was at Winchester on active service, the altar would be an early one, but he may have come in some other capacity, or even on leave, and there is really nothing to date the inscription at all closely. The other point is a notice in a 4th century list of Roman officials of a " Procurator gynaecii in Britannis Ventensis," Administrator of the imperial weaving works at Venta in Britain. Though there were two other Ventas, one in Norfolk, the other in Monmouthshire, neither were suited for sheep grazing. So there must have been a weaving factory at Winchester, perhaps for the supply of clothing to the garrisons of the forts of the Saxon shore which guarded the coast of 4th century Britain. Two of these forts indeed stood not far away, at Portchester and Carisbrooke Castle in the Isle of Wight.

Archaeology has little to tell of Christianity in Roman Britain, but legend has given Winchester a British King Lucius, who shares with several other legendary persons the credit of having introduced Christianity into the country during the 2nd century. The present Cathedral stands, so the legend runs, on the site of his earliest Christian Church. Constantine is said to have added a priestly college, but this story is spoilt by the fact that we are credibly informed that it was built in the 14th century style of mediaeval architecture. At any rate Roman Christianity did not here survive Roman Britain. *Christianity arrives*

So much, or so little, do we know of Venta Belgarum ; no doubt it was once important, like its neighbour Silchester (Calleva Atrebatum), but unlike Silchester it has continued so. A Saxon and a Norman town have sprung up on its remains and obliterated them.

By the early 5th century barbarian raids and Imperial usurpers between them had ruined Roman Britain. Gaul and Rome itself were laid waste, and in 410 came the rescript of Honorius bidding the British cantons look after themselves. The villas and their estates were desolated, the towns were decaying, and while the peasants of the native villages alone still clung to their upland tillage, the country fell piecemeal away from its provincial civilization. Piecemeal likewise there came on it the Angles, the Saxons, and the Jutes. *The Dark Ages*

7

It is from their cemeteries that archaeology can tell us most about the newcomers, and while Jutes and Britons seem to have amalgamated in Kent, the main Anglo-Saxon movement was into the country from the north-east. Thus though archaeology and the Anglo-Saxon Chronicle alike attest early Saxon settlements in Sussex, and Jutes established themselves in the Isle of Wight and the Meon Valley, the earliest Wessex seems to have been on the Upper Thames, and the southern downland, which encloses Winchester, has yielded no certain trace of the Saxons prior to the late 6th century. The Chronicle indeed tells how Cerdic landed at Cerdices Ora in 495, and how he and his son Cynric and his grandson Ceawlin overran the country from this starting-point on or near Southampton Water. We need not reject the records of such roving 'war-bands,' but Cerdic and Cynric are not Saxon names, and after Ceawlin in 571 appeared on the Upper Thames, where Saxons really were settled, his motley followers became significantly called ' Gewissae,' the ' allies.' It was only when such mingled bands of adventurers at last turned to settle the land of the Britons that the ' Saxoniza-tion ' of Wessex can be said to have really begun, and it is not till the 7th century that Winchester becomes the known capital of a West Saxon king.

The Christian mission of Birinus was founded in 634 in the earlier core of Wessex on the Thames at Dorchester, and not till 662 did Bishop Haeddi more the See to Winchester, where a Minster was now built. The land where the forefathers of Birinus' convert King Cynegils had roved must have been British still, suffering doubtless much at times from such bands of freebooters, but yet able to resist determined land-winning invasions.

It is a round half-century before the emergence King Arthur of Ceawlin that, our chronicles tell us, such British resistance secured its greatest successes, associated with the names first of Ambrosius Aurelianus and then of Arthur; and Arthur's battles, culminating in the great victory of Mount Badon, may well be located here in the south country. Thus the mediaeval romances which make Winchester King Arthur's Camelot may contain, unconsciously perhaps, the seeds of truth.

At least the 5th and 6th centuries saw a great The Winchester Bowl revival of Celtic art in Britain, of which enamel-work is the finest embodiment, and in the Celtic-enamelled silver escutcheons of the splendid bronze bowl found in 1930 in a Saxon grave of about 600, dug in the earth bank of Oliver's Battery, we may see one of the last glories of the craftsmanship of Arthurian Winchester, buried as a trophy with the Saxon who had looted it. And the Celtic artistic tradition must have entered into the mingling of races that went to the making of Wessex, to emerge transformed in the inspiration of the famous Winchester School of Late Saxon illumination.

Such, as we can dimly see it, was the formation Winchester Capital of Wessex and England of the kingdom that descended to Egbert, whose triumph over Mercia and Northumbria in 829 made Winchester the capital of England. Here ten years later he was laid to rest :

> "At Wynchestre lyggeth ys bon
> Buried in a marble ston."

Not many years after his death (*c.* 850) arose St. Swithun another, and as great a name. Swithun became Bishop of Winchester. Of his career little is known ; we are told that he wished that, on his death, his bones should be buried outside the

9

Minster so that rain might fall on him and men tread over his head. He left his mark upon the architecture of the city in more ways than one. Under his advice a strong wall of defence was built round the Minster. The present Close wall is still in part built upon its foundations. It was probably this wall which saved the Minster, when in 860 the Danes " destruede Wincestre al out," for we do not hear of them harming the Church. Swithun also built a bridge over the river at the east end of the town. After a simple and a useful life (these Saxon saints were men of action) Swithun died and was buried, as above mentioned. In due course he was canonized, and became the object of reverence of countless pilgrims. Not till later, by the aid of the legend-maker, did he begin to exercise a mysterious influence upon the weather.

Alfred But he has a still greater claim to fame. Under his eye the boyhood of Alfred himself was passed. The latter began to reign in 871 ; and now the great struggle with the Danes had to be fought to the finish. Though driven from his capital, and left almost without an army, he never lost heart, and at length won a great victory at Ethandune, after which he concluded in 878 the famous Treaty of Wedmore or Chippenham. By this agreement, Guthrum, the Danish leader, promised to evacuate Wessex and to accept Christianity. Not long afterwards, however, he was again giving trouble. But Alfred again defeated him, and this time concluded a Treaty (885 or 886), by which England was divided by the line of Watling Street, the Danes keeping the north and east, while Alfred retained his hold over the south and west, including the all-important towns of Winchester and London.

Peace once established, Alfred turned to other things. He encouraged literature and art, himself translating many books into the English tongue, and writing for a time the entries in the Anglo-Saxon Chronicle, which he originated. This was the first history in their own language produced by any of the Teutonic races. It ran, in the Peterborough copy at any rate, from A.D. I to A.D. 1154. Amongst other things he issued a new code of laws, and collected facts about the distribution of land in a register, the *Liber de Winton*, the earliest Domesday Book. This record was kept till the more complete Domesday of the Conqueror rendered it useless. He built ships of war, with which he fought and defeated the Danes in the Solent. Their ships he burnt and sunk in the Hamble River ; a portion of one has been dug out and is now in the Westgate Museum. The prisoners that he captured were perhaps hung over the walls of Wolvesey Palace.

In this Palace he held his court, and we can hardly doubt but that he had to rebuild it after the Danish sack. We cannot say more, for every stone disappeared when this early building made way for the later Norman Palace. There is indeed herringbone masonry near the south-east corner of the wall, but it is probably not Anglo-Saxon. We are upon safer ground when we turn to Alfred's ecclesiastical foundations. ' Old Minster ' attributed to the days of Cynegils already stood on the site of the present Cathedral. To the north of this it was Alfred's intention that there **New Minster** should stand what was to be known as the New **and Nuns'** Minster, which was built by his son Edward the **Minster**

11

Elder. It has disappeared entirely, though, when the road between Dumper's and the Close was built, the outline of the foundations of two western towers could be clearly traced. His will also laid upon his son the burden of providing another establishment for Nuns. Nunnaminster, as it was called, stood to the east of New Minster, that is, between it and the river. The names of Abbey Passage, Abbey House, and Abbey Mill commemorate its existence.

See Plan, p. 12

Alfred was buried in the Old Minster, but the fear of his greatness was too strong, and the story runs that the monks were frightened by the continual walkings of his ghost, and besought Edward to remove his bones into the New Minster then just completed. There we may hope for a while they rested at peace. They were destined to undergo another moving, when the New Minster monks moved to Hyde Abbey (in 1110). At the final destruction of the Monastery ruins a stone carved "Aelfred Rex, DCCCLXXXI," was sold for a mere song to a passing connoisseur. It is now in Corby Castle.

From Ponthieu, in Normandy, meanwhile, came refugees from a Danish raid, bringing with them the bones of St. Judocus, known by the less dignified name of St. Josse. He was readily admitted to the New Minster. His shrine became the centre of devotion, and many miracles were performed there.

St. Dunstan and St. Aethelwold reform the Church

By this time it is evident that Winchester was already becoming what it has indeed been ever since, a great ecclesiastical centre. Both the old and new Minsters had received establishments of "canons," clerics that is, who, though not monks, were supposed to live in common, and to perform the services in the Cathedral

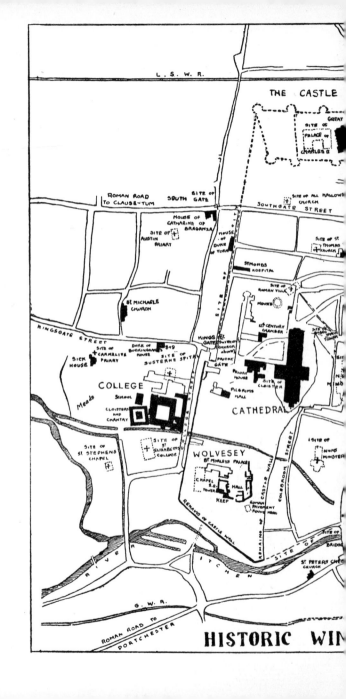

HISTORIC WIN

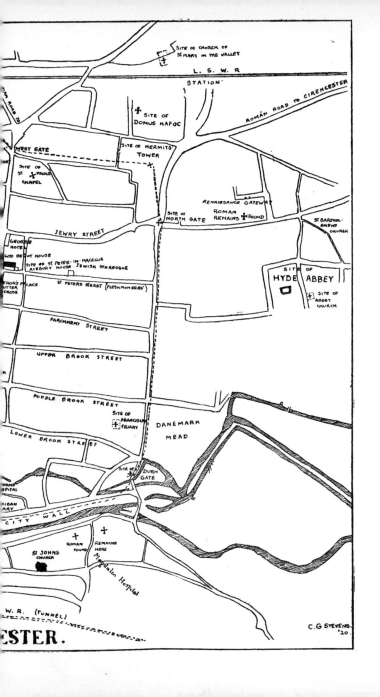

Church. In this particular case, however, they appear to have been rich and easy-going gentlemen, who lived in comfort and luxury on their estates, leaving all their duties to their deputies, " who, poor fellows, worked and starved," and grudging to buy " even a sorry cloth for the altar or a cup worth a few shillings." The need for reform called forth two great figures. One was St. Dunstan, who spent many years at Winchester in his youth, and, as Archbishop of Canterbury must constantly have had occasion to visit the capital. The other was his nominee to the See of Winchester, St. Aethelwold, who worked with him in introducing the severity and efficiency of the monastic life according to the rule of St. Benedict. In 962 he brought matters to a head by ordering these canons to put on monkish garments or lose their places. " In vain," it is said, " they croaked with raven voices, Cras, Cras, To-morrow, To-morrow," for all were turned out except three, and a party of monks who had been waiting outside the door came in and filled their vacant seats. The ejected canons, however, refused to acquiesce in their defeat and appealed to the King. A council was therefore held in the Winchester refectory with Archbishop Dunstan presiding. The canons had little chance of success, and the issue was finally settled against them by the Crucifix on the wall of the refectory, which, with human voice, gave its decision in favour of the newly installed monks. A new régime began. The ways of the monks were stricter and more worthy of the great Orders which brought from the Continent so much strength and piety into the life of the English Church. No more striking memorial exists than the great school of illumination, which throve at Winchester at this time. Here were wrought manuscripts which combined the old Celtic style of intricate interlacings with some inspiration from the Continental artists, and for which the world could then show no match. The famous Benedictional of St. Aethelwold is a gem among these. But the Bishop left for himself more lasting memorials. Like St. Swithun, he interested himself in the welfare of the place, conducting water into the town at great expense by canals like Logie. The draining of the river valley was always a serious problem. But the chief of his works was the rebuilding of the Old Minster upon a splendid and ambitious scale, which will be described later.

The Danes and Canute

Several times the city was threatened with destruction by the Danes. Already as early as 927 it had been besieged. A single combat finally decided the day. Guy, Earl of Warwick, was the Saxon champion, and by the aid of a friendly crow which fluttered in his opponent's face, he came out victorious. " The Danish giant Colebrand in Hyde-meads, by Guy, Earl of Warwick, was struck dead." The spot where the combat See Plan, p. 12 took place near Hyde Abbey is known as Danemark to this day. Now, once again, in 1001, the country was overrun ; Aethelred the Unready was defeated at Alton, and the Danish army marched insultingly by the walls of Winton, which were too strongly defended to be worth attacking. Aethelred's foolish revenge, the order which went forth to massacre all Danes in the land upon St. Brice's Day, brought Swein and his son, Canute, over to avenge their slaughtered kin. Aethelred fled to Normandy, and in due course Canute sat on the throne of England at

14

Winchester. As he had his native kingdom also to control, it was well for him that the city lay near a port, and it was at Southampton that he got his feet wet in order to read his courtiers a lesson. He did his duty by the city, and was a most liberal benefactor of both the Old and New Minsters, presenting to the latter a huge gold and silver cross, which stood upon its altar ; the Old Minster received at his hands " three hides of land called Hille." If this were St. Catharine's Hill the Winchester " Notion " would be at least nine centuries old.* Canute was buried in the Old Minster, and now in one of the chests in the presbytery of the Cathedral (made at a later date by Bishop Fox) repose the bones of our Scandinavian King, together with those of Emma his queen and two bishops.

Thirty years later Edward the Confessor had **The** also passed away, and the English hopes been **Conquest** destroyed with the death of Harold at Hastings. The New Minster monks were true to the national cause ; the abbot, an uncle of Harold's, led them to take their part in the battle. When the Normans were spoiling the slain, they found the abbot and his men lying dead with monk's habits under their mail. William, being informed of this, grimly remarked, " The abbot is worth a barony, and each monk a manor," and made good his words by taking away 20,000 acres of their lands, and refusing to allow the appointment of a new abbot for several years. To complete the intimidation of the monks, he built his Palace

* See *Saint Catharine's Hill, Winchester*, p. 192, note. " Objections to this theory are : (1) three hides is far too large an assessment, the area of the Hill being 100 acres while three hides represents 300 acres ; (2) both Chilcomb and Twyford were Church property from the first, and the hill must have been in one of these parishes."

on the western portion of their site, already uncomfortably small. William had, in fact, decided to accept Winchester as his capital, as it was conveniently situated for Rouen, his Norman capital, more so at least than London. We may conveniently end the history of pre-Norman Winchester with the re-crowning of the Conqueror in the year 1068 in the Old Minster of St. Swithun.

Old Minster   The first Christian church in Winchester was built in the years of conversion in the middle 7th century, and dedicated to St. Peter and St. Paul. In 971 this building was replaced by Bishop Aethelwold's Minster, and soon St. Swithun eclipsed the two apostles. It appears to have been under the special protection of the saint from the first : for it seems that when one Godus had the misfortune to fall from the very top of the structure, a great number of his companions, looking down from above, saw him pick himself up, wondering where he was, find his spade, and continue work. The new church is described in glowing elegiacs by a monk, Wulfstan. If we are to believe him, we must imagine a building so full of chapels, intricate passages, and crowded columns, that a man might easily get lost. Special guides were, as a fact, provided to conduct pilgrims from shrine to shrine. The central tower was crowned with a low pyramidal roof and on the peak of this perched See Plate, an enormous cock. One of the miniatures p. 17 in the Benedictional of St. Aethelwold gives us a vivid picture of this in somewhat doubtful perspective. More wonderful than all was the organ of 400 pipes, for which we are told there

16

A CONJECTURAL VIEW OF SAXON WINCHESTER. CIRCA A.D. 1000. LOOKING EAST

NEW MINSTER   NUNS MINSTER   OLD MINSTER (and WELL for BAPTISM)   CHURCH PATH in ENGLAND   SLOPE BARS to   WOLVESEY and ST
   BY ST ÆTHELWOLD. [Freely based on information   VALLEY   PORTMASTER   CATHARINE HILL
   in the Benedictional of ST ÆTHELWOLD, and existing SAXON Churches.]

C

were seventy blowers, working like galley-slaves in full swing with toil and sweat, and the noise of their shouting as they cheered each other on filled the wind box. " Two brethren play the organ," says the poet, " in unity of spirit, ruling each his own alphabet " (for on every tongue was painted a letter indicating the note), " and when the players pushed in these tongues and set free the sound, forth issued seven jubilant notes. Like thunder the iron voice assaults the ears and drives out every other sound. Nay, so swells the sound that as you hear you must clap your hands to your ears, unable as you draw near to abide the brazen bellowing : all through the city the melody can be heard : and the fame and the echo spread through all lands." As there was no glass in the windows, we can well imagine how disturbing to the monks of the New Minster next door the noise must have been. One suspects that there is ground for the legend that this was not the least of their reasons for migrating (after the Conquest) to the suburbs of Hyde. With such an organ there was only one thing needful to complete this grand new church— a saint to work wonders in competition with St. Josse at the New Minster next door. Very fortunately, just at this time, visions of St. Swithun were seen asking for a change, and the ground was actually seen to heave over his grave outside the church. For all this, when the monks intended to remove his body, the tale runs, that in accordance with the humility of his life, he flatly refused to be moved, weeping tears, and saying that he was unworthy of the honour. This may well be the origin of the tale of forty days' rain, which hindered the removal of his body. As his grave lay just at the Minster door, it can hardly have been due

St.
Swithun's
Bones

18

to climatic conditions. Anyhow, his bones were moved, and were put into a splendid shrine behind the altar.

Like other Anglo-Saxon buildings at Winchester, this great church was doomed to make way for the yet more splendid Norman building ; and indeed, by Walkelin's time, it was in a shaky condition, due either to faulty construction, or else perhaps to the terrific vibrations of the mighty organ. This brings us to the question, " Where precisely did the Anglo-Saxon Cathedral stand in relation to the Norman one, or, if it is preferred, to the present Cathedral ? " (for the latter still preserves in its general features the Norman ground plan). The most important evidence upon this problem is a passage in the *Winchester Annals*, which say, in 1093 (*i.e.*, after the completion of Walkelin's Church), " the monks came from the Old Minster to the new (*i.e.*, to Walkelin's Church), and on St. Swithun's day took up the saint's shrine out of the old church and bore it to the new. Next day, at Walkelin's bidding, they began to break down the old church, and it all came down that year except one porch and the High Altar." Now there are two entirely different solutions to the problem.

Site of the Saxon Minster

(1.) First, the more commonly accepted and at first sight more reasonable of the two. The above extract must convey to the ordinary reader that the old and new buildings stood on different ground. If we examine the present crypt, we find two wells of high antiquity, almost immediately below the High Altar. Now it is well known that the baptistries, or fonts, of early churches used to stand outside the west end of the building. It is, therefore, not unreasonable to suppose that these ancient sacred wells were utilised in that way. It follows that the Anglo-Saxon Church See Plan, p. 48 lay away to the east of these. Now, immediately below the door of the present Lady Chapel, and therefore just east of Walkelin's original chancel, is to be seen in the recesses of the crypt a very unusual mass of masonry, which is declared to be very ancient, perhaps Roman in composition. This may well have been part of the foundation of the west end of the Anglo-Saxon Church of Aethelwold. We should conclude, therefore, that Walkelin started building from the west end of this and continued his church westwards, and on its completion demolished the tottering building that would have blocked its windows to the east— a very reasonable method of setting to work.

(2.) But it has been asserted, with some support of actual evidence, that what he really did was to build the shell of the new church over the old—a church within a church, and that then he demolished the inside structure. In support of this some critics assert that the present crypt is largely Saxon. Now, apart from the unlikelihood of the Saxon substructure being of sufficient stability, or on grand enough a scale to support the colossal weight of the Norman tower piers, there is an interesting piece of archaeological evidence to confute this theory. There is in the crypt a remarkable capital with a very thin square abacus set upon a circular column. This is very rare, but it appears again in the transepts (which are Walkelin's work), and is therefore in all probability of Norman workmanship.

See Plan, p. 48 It is further urged that there is Anglo-Saxon work beneath the North Transept ; and that a mysterious Anglo-Saxon tower, which stood near the north-west corner of the present west end,

20

must have been in close relation to the rest of the Anglo-Saxon building. On this shewing the Anglo-Saxon Church would have been slightly to the north of the Norman, and one fails to see how the theory of a church inside a church would then have been possible. Finally, a most interesting piece of evidence came to light in the digging of the new buttress foundations near the south door of the Nave. A wall several feet below the surface was discovered, running parallel to the wall of the Nave, and then suddenly curving inwards at its western extremity. It has been suggested that this was part of the foundations of the Anglo-Saxon Nave, and that its sweep to the west was a western apse, a feature not uncommon in pre-Norman architecture. Again, however, the " church within a church " theory breaks down, for this wall could not have come within the limits of Walkelin's structure. From this mass of conflicting evidence one returns with some relief to the original theory, which allows one to believe that Walkelin built like any sane man, and not like an Indian carver, enclosing one casket of ivory within another, and to give the chronicler the credit of meaning what he says.

Let us pass to the New Minster of St. Josse, **New Minster** built in 903 by Edward the Elder according to the wishes of his father Alfred. This was built close, too close in fact, to the north side of St. Swithun's. " Between them," we are told, " was but a narrow lane only wide enough for one man to pass along." Another chronicler says, " The singing in one minster conflicted with that in the other, and the ringing of the bells at the same time produced a most horrible discord." Lively competition, not to say some ill-feeling, was a natural result, though we may imagine that these statements are to some extent exaggerated, and probably it was the walls of the monastic buildings and not of the churches which almost touched. In the normal Benedictine plan the Conventual Church occupied the north side of the Cloister, with the Monastic buildings on the other three sides. This arrangement would have brought the Church of the Old Minster next to the Refectory of the New. Of the appearance of the buildings we know nothing beyond the fact that they were of stone, and that a new tower was added in 964.

Nuns'
Minster

Still less is known of the Nuns' Minster. It is said to have had a lofty tower. It was small, and even so its endowment was so slender that it fell into disrepair. King Edward, the Founder, gave it the right of toll over all merchandise passing by land under the east wall and by river under St. Swithun's bridge. This shews that the Itchen was then navigable by ships from the sea.

Of secular buildings, the Castle on the hill by the West Gate may have already existed. We

Wolvesey

know nothing of it. Wolvesey repays study to a greater extent. It stood on an island, as its termination " ey " signifies. The river still flows on its eastern side, and Logie also passes, mainly through gardens and underground, between it and the Cathedral to the west, crossing College Street and flowing through the Warden's garden. It was an excellent position for commanding the river. The discovery of a tesselated pavement shows that the island was inhabited in Roman times. In its great Hall it may well be that Egbert in 829 held the famous council, at which it was decided that the whole realm consolidated under his sway should be known as Angle-land.

Let us imagine the city visited in the last years of Alfred's reign by two French savants, sum- moned from the Continent to the King's court. Shaking off the pursuit of a roving Long-ship of Danes, their vessel runs in under the island of Vectis, and they are glad to disembark on the sedgy flats of Portus Magnus, now a mere shadow of its former self. They might have pursued their course by land or sea to the port of South- ampton and thence up the Itchen by boat or barge, for at least the first part of the overland journey lies through wooded country, and the hills beyond are steep. But they are resolved to push across the Downs by the old Roman road, up hill and See Map at down dale, in a bee-line for their goal ; for end they are well protected by an escort of men- at-arms, who will be more than a match for any dangerous customer, with their stout wooden shields, bronze boss in the middle, and their good battle axes, to say nothing of their captain strutting in a " borrowed " suit of Danish mail. At the end of a long day's march they catch sight, from the last ridge-top, of a conical hill crowned with a breastwork, and below it a huddled mass of buildings in the valley marshes. As they strike down to level ground they pass through tillage ; men with goads are prodding oxen at the plough ; a fat ecclesiastic pays like attentions to a lazy drover. They leave the " Church Farm " upon their right, and come to the riverside, known, like the Portland beach, as Chesill. Boats and barges of every description are moored under the Castle walls, where the ghastly remnants of some Danish captives are hung out *pour encourager les autres*. Just above the mooring place, the bridge of St. Swithun—they will give him a prayer in passing—admits them to the East Gate, and the main street of the town, a poor line of wattled huts, built anew for the most part since the Danish sack in the black days thirty odd years ago. To their left stands the Palace surrounded by water. They pass under a gate into the courtyard, where Alfred, already old at fifty, but always ready to welcome strangers, meets them at his own door. The Palace is largely built of wood, stone being difficult to fetch with the Danes scouring the sea. Nor is its position healthy, for the marshes lie all round, and fever claims its victims among even the royal guests. Yet one can hardly blame the river, if one behaves like Bishop Alphege, who insisted on slipping out at nights, despite the vigilance of the guards, and singing hymns and psalms, standing up to his middle in the river-bed.

The Palace was a busy place. Here the government was carried on. Here the rolls of the Fyrd, or Militia, were kept. The Saxon Domesday Book was not finished yet, and there were hot disputes between " small holders " and the sheriff for royalty to decide. From its watch tower the herald sounds the horn for the monthly " Mote." In another wing the bishop is housed, and is often closeted with the king. One day it will be matters of state, the next some trifling ecclesiastical scandal, a complaint perhaps against the idle priest of the little Saxon church in Headbourne Worthy marshes, who knows not a syllable of Latin, and leaves his " vicar " (curate as we should say) to do all the work. With all these claims upon his time, Alfred still finds opportunity to read and study, or write some translation into English with his own hand. Under his eye in countless cells are workers in gold and metal, illuminators of manuscripts, scribes that copied Anglo-Saxon versions of Latin Fathers, or even wrote at the King's dictation the yearly record in the great *Chronicle*. In the library this impressive tome might be inspected by anyone able to read, and even in the schools of those days they learnt English as well as Latin. It might not however be taken away, for a stout chain held it fast.

The King often worked far into the night. Only after dinner did he allow himself the relaxation of a little music. Grimbald, the monk from Gaul, sang songs of his own country, and Alfred would answer with an Anglo-Saxon battle song to the accompaniment of his own harp.

There lay many a warrior : slain by the spear.
There lay the Northmen : shot over the tops of their shields ;
And there were the Scots : weary and sad.

*   *   *   *

Greater bloodshed : in this island
Has never been seen : before this day,
As the books tell us : as the old writers say,
Since the time when there came : the Angles and the Saxons,
From the east : over the broad seas : to England.

Then he would call Dubslane, Macbetha, and Maclinnan, the three men who came in an open boat all the way from Ireland to hear the wisdom of our Saxon Solomon (though their frail craft was only held together by two and a half skins), and having drunk deep of mead they would entertain the company with ghastly tales of their land beyond the sea.

It was equally instructive after the banquet to visit the refectory of the monks, where milk and carraway-seed loaf were the staple diet. Not but what there were occasions of better fare and clerics who made the most of them. Reformation was much needed, but too often the would-be reformer had to be content with venting in bad

Latin verses his disapproval of some jolly bishop, *nulla laboris agens, pocula multa bibens.*

The " hours " were daily read in the Minster, and " plain song " chanted in Latin. In their shrine of silver and gold the bones of St. Birinus were reverenced daily and exhibited yearly. But as yet St. Swithun rested in peace under the eaves outside. Converts were brought in from time to time to be baptised at the well-head under the west front. They were often lukewarm Danish candidates following the example of King Guthrum, who had been baptised with Alfred as his godfather. Within, under the great stone Rood, the priest is waiting to give absolution to all who wish to receive it, even as in later days Alphege did to Dunstan near this very spot, on that celebrated occasion when Satan, seeing these two precious heads together, attempted one of his " aerial tricks," casting on them a great stone from the sky. To his great chagrin, it should be added, he missed them both, the stone passing between them. But this has no place in the story of our travellers, which is already growing wearisome.

The Mediaeval Period

DURING the Anglo-Saxon period we have seen Waning Winchester as the Royal City, the capital of importance England, and the centre of religion and learning. in Century It was also a commercial centre, ranking as equal before the with London, and the weight standards of Win- Conquest chester regulated the trade of most of southern England. But, in spite of Canute's use of it as capital of his almost imperial domain, a change was already taking place towards the end of that period. Edgar in 958 was hallowed as King of Wessex, not at Winton, but on the banks of the Thames, at a spot which thus earned the name of Kingston. When Edward the Confessor came to the throne, though crowned at Winchester he associated himself almost entirely with Westminster. By way of compensation he organised more completely the " wearing of the crown " at Winchester and Gloucester, as well as London. This annual ceremony consisted in a state progress through the town, a form of re-coronation and a banquet. This went on till Henry I's reign, when it was discontinued, and Winchester then fell definitely into a subordinate position. Instead of being Edward's capital, the city became the stronghold of Earl Godwin, the most powerful man in England, and the leader of the English party in the state as opposed to the King's Norman favourites. In 1053 Godwin came to an end in the dramatic way described by Lytton in *Harold*. He was dining at the royal banquet in the Castle Hall. " May this crumb of bread choke me," said the Earl to the King, " if I am guilty of thy brother's blood." And with that he rolled over in a fit and expired.

On the 5th of January, 1066, Edward died, and Harold was crowned in Westminster Abbey : on the 14th of October he lay dead on the field of Hastings.

William I makes his Head= quarters at Winchester

Winchester submitted quickly to William, cowed by the awful disaster, and before long William made his headquarters here ; for, as has been said above, so long as the King of England was also Duke of Normandy, Winchester was handy for Rouen, and also William, as King of the English, was pre-eminently King of the West Saxons.

Here in the little area, bounded by the High Street, Great Minster Street, and the two Minsters, Old and New, he set up the seat of government. Here were the treasury, the mints, and the standards of weights and measures ; though the Castle at the top of the High Street was his stronghold, he kept his state in the new Palace that he built himself. It has nearly all been swept away. Part of the stonework under the archway by the Butter Cross was probably a support of the royal stables. In the cellars of the sweet shop and several other shops near by, and in the vaults under the town museum, portions of the substructures may still be seen.

See Plan, p. 12

On Whit Sunday, 1068, William was solemnly crowned here with Matilda. The ceremony is said to have been far finer than that in London. A great banquet followed, when a champion rode into the hall clad in full armour, and challenged anyone to deny that William was truly King. This practice was only discontinued in King William IV's reign. None accepted the challenge at the time ; but subsequently various con-spiracies arose, notably that of Waltheof, the last English earl, assisted by two Norman barons. The conspiracy was suppressed ; the two Normans

Earl Waltheof

fled, but Waltheof, betrayed by his Norman wife, was arrested, and though at first forgiven, was brought to Winchester, tried before the Witan, and condemned to death. " When the sentence was once passed," so runs the story, " its execution did not long linger, and while the citizens were still in their beds, Earl Waltheof was summoned to his fate. It was feared that if men knew the deed that was doing, they would rise up and rescue the champion of England. The Earl was led forth to St. Giles' Hill, arrayed in all the badges of his Earl's rank. When he reached the place of martyrdom, he distributed them among the few spectators. He then knelt down to pray aloud, but the headsman, anxious to get the business over before the people could interfere, let fall the sword, and the last earl's head rolled on the ground. Men said that the severed head audibly finished the prayer— ' Libera nos a malo.' " He was buried in Crowland Abbey, and is said to have worked many miracles there.

On that day, no doubt, and on many others Cbe Cown during the years immediately succeeding the under the Conquest, the citizens of Winchester must have Conqueror groaned beneath the yoke of a foreign ruler, and looked back with longing hearts to the days of good King Edward. But as time went on, and they began to reap the blessings of the good government and rigid justice of King William, their hearts became softened, and they settled down to enjoy the manifold advantages which flowed to them from the close connection now maintained with Rouen and the Continent, the stern suppression of internal disorder at home, and the protection afforded by the King's officers to merchants and pilgrims. Trade, encouraged by the wise regulations of the Normans, soon began to flourish. The Castle at the West Gate commanded the town, and its presence protected the city from the attacks of the lawless barons of the neighbourhood, as well as forcing the citizens themselves to live in peace and order. A new and better coinage was issued from the Royal Mints in the Palace Vault (possibly also in St. Thomas' Street, where a Norman cellar marks the probable site of one such Mint), while the severest penalties, mutilations, and the like, were enforced on those who clipped or otherwise tampered with the currency. This all made for the interests of the city, and of stable conditions of trade. No doubt the citizens resented the building of the Royal Palace in their very midst, for the King's presence in the Middle Ages was always regarded as an expensive luxury, an excess of which became a burden upon the resources of the neighbourhood. They were, however, exempted from that crowning indignity, the Domesday Survey. Walkelin, the new bishop, a cousin of the Conqueror, pulled down the old Saxon Minster of St. Aethelwold, and set about building a new Cathedral to the west in the Norman style. No doubt the townsmen at first regretted their old church, but before long they became attached to the new one with its stately arches, massive towers, and fine timber roof, while the hordes of pilgrims who flocked to Winchester to lay their offerings before the shrine of St. Swithun brought plenty of gain to the astute traders of the city.

Rufus   All the more they learned to respect the stern justice of the Conqueror when they felt the rigid tyranny of his son, and the new Chancellor, Ranulf Flambard, builder of Christchurch Priory and Durham Cathedral. It is true that trade prospered, encouraged by the fair which the King granted to be held each year upon St. Giles' Hill. But there were probably few who felt much sorrow when the King's stark body was brought into Winchester " in the crazy two-wheeled cart of a charcoal-burner, drawn by a sorry nag." It had come from the New Forest by the lane from Silkstede, still known as the King's Lane. The body was buried under the central tower of Walkelin's church, which in 1107 fell down. Although some wiseacres held that its constructions were faulty all along, the citizens were firmly convinced that Providence had asserted itself. Rufus' tomb seems to have been moved by his nephew, Bishop Henry de Blois, to a position nearer the altar. It is true that on one of the mortuary chests on Fox's screens in the choir is an inscription telling us that Rufus' bones are contained in it, but against this is the very strong evidence which was found in the tomb already mentioned in front of the altar. Among the relics discovered in it, when it was opened in 1868, were the skeleton of a man of small stature, but great physical strength, and aged about forty, some fragments of cloth of gold and braid of distinctly Norman character, various ornaments, and above all several fragments of wood, which when joined together formed a shaft about three feet in length, and what was possibly an arrow-head. Now the skeleton exactly fits what we know of Rufus, while we are told by an old chronicle that Tyrrell's fatal arrow was buried in the King's stiffened side when he was laid to rest in the Cathedral. This seems conclusive evidence that Rufus' remains are in the Norman tomb with the top of Purbeck marble, and not in any of the mortuary chests. For some unexplained reason the Norman tomb was transferred after the investigation of its contents in 1868 to a position in the Retro-Choir, where it remained until it was moved once more by Dean Kitchin to its present and probably original position under the tower.

Henry I Of the reign of Henry I we cannot say much here. He deserves to rank among the greatest of our kings, for England prospered under his wise rule, and Winchester was not behind in the advantages she drew from the good order he maintained, and the justice impartially administered by his officers. This city had many personal associations with the King. Here he and his English Queen Maud, whom he took out of the nunnery at Romsey, often kept their court. Here, too, as he sat in the Castle Hall, he received the dreadful tidings that his only son had been drowned in the *White Ship*. This awful catastrophe left as the King's heir a daughter, Matilda, for whom he was extremely anxious to secure the throne. She, however, was rendered unpopular by her haughtiness and overbearing manners, while her husband, the Count of Anjou, was only less odious in the eyes of the English barons than the lady herself. But she had an infant son who, she was determined, should sit upon the throne of England, a project which she at length succeeded in carrying out, for he became in 1154 King Henry the Second.

Before that nearly twenty years of anarchy had to be endured, for between this child and the crown of England stood his two cousins, nephews of Henry I: their names were Stephen and Henry de Blois. Stephen was first in royal title alone ; his brother, the Bishop of

Winchester, was in all respects the finer man ; he had all the brains, the ambition, and the firmness of will that Stephen lacked. Had fate bestowed on Henry the crown, on Stephen the mitre, the course of events might have been far different.

This Henry de Blois, who became Bishop in 1129, in the height of his powers, has been very variously judged by posterity ; but he is admittedly one of the most important figures of the century, and perhaps is one of the best representatives of a prevalent type of churchman in the Middle Ages. As one of the two or three most remarkable of the Bishops of Winchester he merits special attention. Henry de Blois

One need not suppose that he entered the Church from any motives of piety ; he may have had no choice in the matter ; indeed, this supposition is borne out by the statement of Giraldus Cambrensis that he was a monk of Cluny from his very boyhood. Therefore it is not surprising that in the flower of his age he expressed all those virile characteristics of strength of mind and far-reaching ambition which cannot be suppressed by the accident of ecclesiastical position ; what rather is remarkable is that he should ever, even in his latter and more sober years, have attained to the degree of piety, which all chroniclers attest and which was so much more becoming than usual in a mediaeval prelate.

The key to his policy during all the troubled years that followed the death of Henry I was the advancement and improvement of the bishopric of Winchester. To attain this end he made capital out of every situation and improved every opportunity : now declaring himself for one party, now for the other, now temporising between the two, he pursued his aim with steadfast fixity of purpose. To do him justice, he always had a real sense of the dignity and interest of the Church at large, which, as time and age softened his character, effaced the personal considerations which were at first dominant.

At first, however, he was all for the things of this world ; he strengthened his position as best he might by intriguing, and building castles : Matthew Paris states that in the single year 1138 he was engaged in building six castles (of which Merdon, Waltham, Farnham, and Wolvesey are near enough to be fairly familiar to us), yet it is significant of the complexity of his character that at the same time St. Cross, which is a nobler memorial to him than all his castles, was being built.

To secure not only his power but his safety in these troublous times, he must make what speed he might in his fortification of the episcopal palace of Wolvesey, probably since late Saxon times assigned to the Bishop. The uneven courses and general inferiority of the masonry in the upper parts of the wall betray the haste in which the stronghold was completed. His brother, of whom he was a not invariable supporter, had objected to the almost universal building of castles, and attacked two prelates for this offence. Henry, who was always strong for the privileges of the Church, resented his action, and had the audacity to summon him to a council at Winchester ; and to the astonishment of all present produced a Papal Bull nominating himself as Legate. The result of the Council was a compromise, but Henry and a great part of the Churchmen were alienated by Stephen ; so in the next year, when the tide of success was rising for

34

Matilda, Henry de Blois, hoping that he might profit by making a virtue of necessity, acknowledged her as ruler without much ado. Much as he did then to promote her interests, she soon estranged him from her cause by her intractable and proud behaviour.

Winchester was now in the forefront of the struggle. After the failure of a characteristic device for entrapping the principal adherents of Matilda in Winchester, Henry broke into open revolt. Matilda got possession of the castle on the hill and a duel of bombardment ensued, as a result of which a disastrous conflagration spread over a great part of the town, destroying many churches, the Nuns' Minster and even Hyde Abbey, the new foundation of New Minster without the walls. The fire must therefore have taken a great hold on the city and incidentally completed the destruction of the Conqueror's Palace, already damaged by a previous fire in 1103. This was very convenient for Henry, but there is no particular reason for supposing it to have been deliberately caused by him. The stone of the Palace was used for the completion of the Keep at Wolvesey, and its site was assigned to St. Lawrence's Church.

After many misfortunes Stephen's reign came to a tardy pacification and an unlamented close. During these years his brother was concerned in an attempt to convert the Bishopric of Winchester into an Archbishopric embracing seven south-western dioceses. This aspiration, which was not uncommon in mediaeval bishops, was very nearly realised, for Pope Lucius II was prevailed upon to send him a Pall, but on account of the " general murmur " he was forced to withdraw his pretensions.

35

In 1142 at a Council he had, as Legate, declared ploughs and ploughmen inviolable. This protection of agriculture from the damages of war shows signs of some sense even in those times of anarchy. After the accession of Henry II he thought himself in danger, so, transferring his treasures to France, he fled. The King thereupon took advantage of the occasion to destroy three of his adulterine castles. The great bishop soon returned to his country and to an honoured and important position in its counsels ; but he was never again the first man in England.

In his latter years he renounced the aspirations of this world and put on the austere humility and piety proper to a monk of Cluny : his benefactions were very liberal : for the Cathedral he built a Treasury, at the meeting of the nave and south transept ; he collected various relics, and the most remarkable of his gifts is the black Font.

True to his old principles, he supported Thomas of Becket to the end of his days, and died " a prophet new inspired " of woe to King Henry.

So ended one of the first men of his age ; in the words of his chronicler, " may his soul lie in Abraham's bosom."

Henry II   The further history of Matilda we need not pursue, except to record that it was from Winchester that she accomplished her celebrated escape in a leaden coffin borne on the shoulders of her men. As we have said, she succeeded in her ambition, and her son, Henry II, sat on the throne, and inherited an empire stretching from the Tweed to the Pyrenees. There was seldom a young man less lucky in his relatives, or more lucky as their heir. He reformed the law of the land, and, what is more, enforced it. He tried to reform the Church, and would have done that

36

too but for the outcry after Becket's death. Such tasks, as well as an extensive empire, called him elsewhere than Winchester ; the wearing of the crown was discontinued, and we do not find him in the old capital for a space of twenty years. The fact was that London had taken its place. This change was, so to speak, clinched by the succession of an absentee King. Richard was seldom in Winchester, for he was seldom in England, the Crusades being now in full swing. Crusades Many a cavalcade must have ridden out from the Hostel of the Knights of St. John of Jerusalem, See Plan, near the East Gate, and, taking their way to p. 12 Southampton, have passed out to the Holy Land. For a brief period after his imprisonment on the Continent, King Richard was once more in England, and in 1195 he was crowned a second time in the Cathedral here, and after hearing mass from a great throne in the Nave, he repaired to the monks' quarters for dinner. It is said that wine was served from the fine vaulted hall that is still standing on the west side of the Close, built into the house with the new verandah-porch. But this restless King was soon off again to France, where he died a year before the century closed.

The turn from the twelfth to the thirteenth The English century was marked by the growth, gradual Revival indeed, but shewing itself in many ways, of a new national spirit. The country was, in a word, beginning to find itself to be *England*—no longer a loose confederacy of jealous Saxon states, nor the conquered province of a Norman duke. It exhibited this spirit in no uncertain manner throughout the first half of the thirteenth century, resenting the draining of English pockets for foreign purposes, whether for Jerusalem or Rome, resenting the introduction of foreign favourites at the court and in the administration of the country, and, finally, claiming with Simon de Montfort that England should be for the English. In nothing did this new spirit shew itself more clearly than in architecture. There grew up about the turn of the century a new style, which is rightly termed Early English, and which was in every way the direct opposite of the old Norman style, pointed where that had been round, light and airy where that had been ponderous and dark. It may seem fanciful to see in its soaring arches the fresh life and aspirations of a people gradually released from the heavy yoke of the Early Norman kings. But the fact remains that the builders of this time took a quite undeniable delight in undoing the Norman work. In particular they insisted in sweeping away the apses, or rounded ends of the chancels, which are, on this account, so rare in England, though so common on the Continent. The great Early English builder at

Bishop Godfrey de Lucy

Winchester was Bishop Godfrey de Lucy, 1189—1204. We will not stop now to discuss his work in detail, but it should be mentioned that he entirely transformed the eastern end of the

See Plan, p. 48

Cathedral behind the High Altar. So we have in those fragile arches a record in stone, as it were, of the new era that was beginning, when as yet it wanted twenty years to the signing of Magna Charta. One cause for this rebuilding of the eastern end was that the confined space of the Norman Ambulatory (as they called the passage behind the High Altar) was inadequate for the crowd of pilgrims that now visited St. Swithun's shrine, which stood under the centre of de Lucy's vaulted Retro-choir till the Reformation swept it away.

De Lucy died in 1204, and was succeeded by **Henry III.** Peter des Roches, a villain and a foreigner : **Bishop Peter** under John and Henry III he was the evil genius **des Roches** of Winchester. It happened also that Winchester enjoyed once more at this time a brief return of royal favour. This was due to the accident that Henry III was born at Winchester, and christened possibly in Henry de Blois' font. What is more, he remembered the fact, and to the end of his days retained a peculiar affection for the place of his birth. Many Wintonians must have bitterly regretted this fancy of his ; but none more than the monks. It was not merely the presence of his French-speaking favourites that disgusted them. These they would have suffered gladly, had he not persisted in an attempt to force his own nominees upon the unwilling House of St. Swithun ; Peter des Roches had left the country in disgrace, and they did not want another Peter. By ejecting the disobedient monks, by even tearing them from the High Altar of the Cathedral and locking them up in the dungeon out- **See Frontis-** side the West Gate (which was originally the Hawk **piece, No. 14** House of the King's Park), the King succeeded at last in enforcing his wishes. He added insult to injury by actually preaching them a sermon, and his text was " Righteousness and peace have kissed each other " !

If Henry quarrelled with the monks he got on well with the citizens, with whom as a native of their town and a constant visitor, he was naturally popular ; and they habitually welcomed him on his arrival by hanging out curtains and carpets.

This all led to a sort of town and gown rivalry **Simon de** between the High Street and the Close, which **Montfort** developed in the stormy days of Earl Simon's **and the** revolt into open warfare, the religious party **Civil War**

39

See Plan, p. 12

supporting, of course, the rebellious Nationalists. Kingsgate was the scene of the hottest conflict, the point where the town walls and Close walls coincide. At a rumour that the monks intended to admit Earl Simon's men through the Kingsgate, the citizens rushed down St. Swithun's Street between the two walls, and assaulted fiercely the Close gate at the bottom. They set fire to it, and burnt down Kingsgate into the bargain. The gate was later rebuilt, and the little church above was used by the lay attendants of the House of St. Swithun.

Position of the City

Still the town did not lose favour in the royal eyes. Prince Edward, later known as Edward I, starting for the Crusades, was blessed in the Chapter House, where those old Norman pillars now stand, before he sailed from Southampton to join St. Louis of France, the finder of the true Crown of Thorns. Henry III himself had a special fancy for eating his Christmas dinner in the town of his birth, especially when he was entertained at the Bishop's expense at Wolvesey. This experiment was so entirely to his mind that he repeated it in the following year. Indeed, Winchester still ranked next after London in importance ; and when David, brother of Llewellyn of Wales, was " quartered," and his head exhibited at London, our city successfully maintained her claim to the privilege of having his right shoulder Perhaps a less gruesome incident throws even more light on her status. At a celebration to the memory of Edward the Confessor at Westminster, both Wintonians and Londoners laid claim to the office of cup bearers. When the Londoners withdrew in a huff, our more prudent and possibly more hungry forefathers stayed behind and finished the meal !

On Henry's death, Winchester relapsed into the position of a provincial Windsor. Yet even so she maintained an importance of her own : she remained a great ecclesiastical city. The place must have been as full of habited monks and tonsured clerics as a market town is of farmers on a fair day. Hundreds of novices must here have taken vows, not inconsolable at forfeiting their liberty in exchange for not only the protection of the sanctuary against the lawless violence of the times, but also for that immunity from the heavy hand of the law which Becket died to secure for them. An Ecclesi=astical Centre

What this city was like we can gather from the *Domesday of Winton*, which Henry I caused to be compiled about 1113. The Conqueror had omitted his capital from the original Domesday, and this record fills that gap. Even so we learn little from it of the churches or church lands, for the commissioners dealt only with King's land. High Street, now as always, was the centre of city life. Here the commissioners started their work. It went by the name of Cyp Street, which is the same word as Cheap-side, and about the centre it was known more particularly as Callis Regis, or Kingsway. Starting at the northeast corner of the city, the quarter occupied by a colony of tanners and fullers, and other poor trades, they came first to an important building at the lower end of the High Street. This was the Knights' Hall, a club and guardroom for the young men, pages, and nobles. They seem to have formed a guild or company which had charge of the protection of the city. This guild may, as at London, have been the origin of the City Corporation. Adjoining this was the Chapel of St. John, in connection with a Hostel of the The High Street See Frontispiece, No. 4

41

Knights of St. John of Jerusalem. This was built at a slightly later date than the enquiry of the commissioners, in the pointed Early English style with plain lancet windows. It survives as a wing of St. John's Rooms. After passing a block of poor houses, the commissioners next came to the prison house, and the lodging of the eight carnifices or King's executioners, also on the north side of the street and facing the Conqueror's Palace. Then came the "Domus Godbiete," or God Begot House. This name appears to derive from the nickname of a certain Elfric, called the "Goodsgetter." Queen Emma, Ethelred's wife, who was the next owner of the house, had given it to the monks of St. Swithun's with a charter, which rendered it outside all civil authority. Any felon in fact could "byde and dwelle there safe from eny maner officer," which was not a pleasant state of affairs for the police of the city. The building, as it now stands, is mainly of a far later date, but it retained these remarkable privileges for over five centuries. Just above it was Earl Godwin's house, and opposite, the Old Guildhall, where the clock now hangs. Here the Guild of Merchants held their meetings. These worthies came to have a very important say in the administration of the town ; for instance, it was they who elected the members of Parliament. The George may have stood at the corner even then. St. Peter's-in-the-Shambles stood behind Godbegot House, and rows of butchers' shops that gave the church its name. There the curfew was rung nightly. Quite near to it was another place of worship, the Jewish synagogue. The Jews were always highly favoured at Winchester, which one of them describes as a very "Jerusalem" of the north ; and the name of

Jewry still clings to the quarter which was assigned to them. The general impression that one gets from the survey is that the houses were few and the population small, eight or nine thousand probably. Much of the space within the walls was taken up with gardens, churches, and their closes. But, though small, the population was rich and flourishing. The street names tell of prosperous trades. The names point to an odd variety of race : among the old English names appear many Scandinavian, French, Norman, Jewish, and not a few nondescript. Of the defences of the city, more must be said later. They were strong, no doubt, but not so strong as later kings rendered them. A great fosse surrounded the walls, easily filled with water, which was only too abundant in the town. The lower part of the place was a network of streams, and on one occasion the whole floor of a church had to be raised four feet to clear the water.

It is time we turned to the buildings which still exist, and now the story becomes difficult and complicated, though full of interest. The plan given on page 12 will help to elucidate the problems of the various additions and reconstructions.

First, the Cathedral itself. At the time of the **Walkelin's** Conquest there were three great churches close **Cathedral** together : St. Swithun's, the New Minster and the Nuns' Minster. All were doomed to disappear : St. Swithun's was rebuilt : the New Minster was flooded out and abandoned during Henry I's reign : the Nuns' Minster was burnt in the fight between Matilda and de Blois. The first Norman Bishop was Walkelin ; and he was no exception to his time. The last years of the eleventh century saw an unprecedented amount

43

of church-building. All over the country great churches were rising, and so important a town as Winchester could not be left behind : Walkelin began work in 1079, and finished in 1093. The first part he built was the crypt. This is of unusual detail : and a theory has been put forward that it was itself destined to be the church, but this can hardly be so, considering its height. It contains several interesting features. There are two wells, one of them probably Roman, the other called after St. Birinus, the missionary of Wessex. The walls are of great thickness : and the capitals form an interesting series, illustrating their development in Norman times. First they have a plain abacus, then an abacus and a small cushion. Later the cushion itself developed into the flowery, carved decoration we usually see on pillars. The arches themselves are in one place of a most unusual twisted shape owing to their place in the apse, and they have no keystone. The east end of the crypt is far later, being de Lucy's work of about 1200.

The Crypt

Walkelin built his church on a marsh, using wooden piles as foundation. When the marsh was drained quite recently, these piles were probably affected : at any rate substantial repairs to the foundations were completed in 1912. Above ground he built in the Norman fashion, which was to construct two thin walls and fill the space between with rubble. The masonry was therefore only skin deep : this meant that it was neither very durable nor very strong, and it probably accounts for the collapse of the central tower and the bad state of the two western ones when they were pulled down. For when Walkelin built his Cathedral it was forty feet longer than

44

it is to-day, and the west end included two transepts, surmounted by great towers. The length See Plan p. 48 of the front was 128 feet ; and all that remains of it to-day is a short stretch of masonry in the wall which separates the garden of one of the Close houses from the passage at the south-west corner of the Cathedral. It must have been very majestic, although somewhat plain and formal : it probably resembled the Abbaye aux Hommes at Caen. When it was pulled down by Edyngton, the stone was used to pave Kingsgate Street.

The Nave has been entirely transformed by **The Nave** William of Wykeham and little can be said about it. It was built in three storeys of nearly equal size, and can best be imagined by looking at the transepts. The lowness of the arch can best be See Diagram, p. 48 seen by the two extant Norman capitals on the first and second columns from the choir-screen on the north side. The height of the triforium arch can be seen by looking at the arch above Wykeham's chapel from the north. The round Norman outline can be clearly seen. The last point about the Nave is that it did not have a flat roof, such as the transepts still possess, but a pitched one. The result would have been more lofty than Wykeham's vault of stone. The beams can still be seen by anyone who cares to climb up above the vaulting. All the wood is oak and comes from Hampage Wood. William the Conqueror granted Walkelin as much as he could cut in three days : the bishop collected workmen and took it all, except for one tree, the Gospel Oak, under which St. Augustine preached. William was astonished and swore profusely " by the splendour of God " when he discovered the disappearance of this " delectable wood." The stone came from Quarr in the Isle of Wight, and

45

was well chosen, for it has endured. In the bay to the west of the present choir screen there probably stood the pulpitum, a stone screen which divided the choir from the nave, while one bay further west was the Rood, a great silver Crucifix with the silver figures of St. John and the Virgin which Queen Emma gave to the Old Minster. On the Head of Christ was the golden crown presented by Canute after the famous seashore episode. The arrangement of the pulpitum is a matter of conjecture, but it seems the best way of accounting for the Norman capitals left visible halfway up Wykeham's piers. Some authorities connect them with Edyngton's chapel and that of Adam de Orlton, his predecessor, which may have occupied a corresponding place on the north side. In the absence of any accepted suggestion, the pulpitum theory, although pure invention, seems as good as any other.

The Transepts The transepts have already been spoken of as the only large portion of surviving Norman. The galleries which fill their ends were probably designed for marshalling processions before they went round the triforium. A screen or some other object may have crossed the front of these galleries, which would account for the otherwise inexplicable stopping short of the pillars on either side halfway to the roof. The Treasury in the south transept was built by de Blois, who also gave the black font in the Nave. In the Treasury there were found a short time ago two stone-lined pits in the floor : it has been suggested that they once held the bones now in the mortuary chests above the Choir.* The external effect of

* It is much more probable, as Canon Goodman suggests, that these pits were used as money-chests. The Cathedral was obliged by Statute to keep £200 as cash in hand.

the transepts is rather disappointing. This is partly due to the insertion of Perpendicular tracery in some of the windows by William of Wykeham, and partly to the fact that they were not completed. The strengthening at the corners seems to indicate that two turrets were intended to flank the gables on each side. The outside appearance of the church must have been very different. The Choir ended in an apse with a round ambulatory : the aisles finished squarely and probably carried towers, for their foundations are unnecessarily strong. There were then five towers altogether—two at the west end, two at the east end and one at the crossing, and four turrets on the transepts ; and this must have helped to relieve the flat severity of the long nave. The south side of the Nave, if we except Wykeham's window tracery and the ten new buttresses, is a fair specimen of the external Norman workmanship. The latest Norman work **The** in the Cathedral is the Central Tower, which had **Central** to be rebuilt in 1107 when Walkelin's tower fell **Tower** down. It shows a considerable improvement in style. It is interesting to note how much of the transepts the tower destroyed in falling, which can easily be done by comparing the mortar. The old Norman has a far thicker and coarser mortar : it is frequently as much as an inch thick between the stones. The new builders used a finer and stronger material, and obtained a far neater effect ; also the carving on the tower windows contrasts with the naked square-edged windows of the earlier work. This time they were determined the tower should not fall down. It was set on four enormous piers of great strength and solidity. They measure over twenty feet from east to west, the size of quite a large

47

room, but less from north to south. This was designed to give strength without blocking the view up the Nave. It must always be remembered that the Normans meant the tower for a lantern : that is to say they meant the inside to be seen, and not vaulted up. By ascending to the belfry one can still see the richly carved windows which were intended to shed light into the Choir. So much for the Norman work : we must now see how it has been changed into the Cathedral of to-day.

Lucy's Alterations

Godfrey de Lucy was Bishop from 1189 till 1204. His alterations have already been mentioned : he started behind the High Altar, and instead of the old Norman apse with square side aisles, he built a large retro-choir. At the end of that he built three similar chapels in a row. Two of them are almost the same : the Guardian Angels' Chapel with its fine painted vault, its magnificent carving, unfortunately concealed by the altar and its fine monument by Le Sueur, and Bishop Langton's Chapel, which has been slightly altered. But the Lady Chapel has been lengthened by a bay, the work of Prior Hunton (about 1500). This makes Winchester the longest mediaeval Cathedral in the world, and the longest Cathedral in England. Liverpool will one day be longer ; but it is noteworthy that whereas Walkelin built his church in sixteen years, Liverpool will take about sixty years in all. In the centre of the retro-choir stood the gorgeous shrine of St. Swithun. Its position has been suggested by the existence of a hole in the centre of one of the bosses of the vaulting, which may have been used for a pulley to raise the lid of the shrine. This would make its position mid-way between the chapels of Beaufort and

Waynflete. Moreover, until a short time ago there was a line of depression at the west ends of these chapels and between them which might have been caused by many kneeling pilgrims. Many pilgrims came to visit this shrine, and their route has been mapped out, although much of it is pure hypothesis. They entered at a door in the north transept, which is now blocked up, but is easily visible from outside. Immediately opposite this door, above the monument to S. S. Wesley, is a dark triangular shadow : here, it is very plausibly suggested, was an image of St. Christopher, the patron saint of travellers. Below it was a box for alms whose iron supports are concealed by the same memorial tablet. Just by in the Chapel of St. Sepulchre is a quatrefoil-shaped embrasure. The bottom of this is worn smooth while the top is still rough ; inside is an iron spike ; here it is suggested that a flame was always burning, from which the pilgrims might light the candles that they carried round with them as they proceeded to pay their devotions at the shrine. The reliquary of St. Swithun was reconstructed about 1250 from an earlier work of 971, made when the Saint's bones were brought inside. It was a favourite meeting-place for pilgrims from the West on their way to Canterbury. By the end of the fifteenth century it had lost its importance. In 1538 Thomas Wriothesley destroyed it by the order of Henry VIII's minister, Cromwell. In order to prevent intrusion into their quarters, the monks placed a pair of ironwork gates in the south aisle of the Choir. These gates are still there and are one of the finest examples of mediaeval ironwork in the country and well deserve attention.

Lucy did not alter the Norman Choir, but it was not destined to remain. Some time during the fourteenth century it went the way of the Norman ambulatory and apse. Unpolished Purbeck columns and Decorated arches took its place. Bishop Fox finished it off by substituting Perpendicular choir-aisles for the old Norman ones. This long description can hardly be clear without reference to the plan (p. 48) : for the whole eastern limb of the church is a remarkable jumble of different styles. It is interesting, however, that all the later builders have been forced to employ the Norman foundations. This has the result that the end of the Choir still turns inwards as if for an apse. It ends neither round nor square but in a coffin shape. This is partly concealed by the chapels of Fox and Gardiner, but the converging lines of columns can be clearly seen from the Retro-choir.

Monastic Buildings

South of the church was the cloister, surrounded by the monastic buildings ; of these, unfortunately, very little remains, but they deserve some mention. First, then, there was the cloister itself, probably, like most other Norman cloisters, built of wood. Opening on to its east and west walks respectively were two doors in the nave of the church. These were used by the monks in the procession at High Mass on Sundays, when they passed out of the church by the eastern door, made the round of the claustral buildings, and entered the church again by the western door. Both these doors are now blocked up ; indeed there are no less than three doors at the western end, all of them now filled in, of which the easternmost probably occupies the position of the original western processional door.

Throughout See Diagram, p. 48

50

Of the buildings themselves, the one adjoining the south transept of the church still remains. This was the Slype, the whole appearance of which has been considerably spoilt by the modern masonry which it was found necessary to put there during the repair of the Cathedral between 1905 and 1912 to support the south wall of the transept. Next to the Slype was the Chapter House ; of it nothing remains save the fine Norman arches which form the entrance, and the pillars of which are supposed to be of Roman origin. It was probably a rectangular building jutting out some way to the east, and possibly terminating in an apse, in which would be a seat for the Prior, while the brethren occupied stone benches round the walls. The Chapter **Chapter** House was a place of prime importance in every **House** monastery : in it the Convent met every day for the reading of a Chapter from the Rule, and for the discussion of business concerning the whole house ; the hinge to which was fixed the seat of the Chapter messenger may still be seen in the masonry below the Norman arches. In addition, however, to the more ordinary uses, the Chapter House at Winchester witnessed many scenes of great historical interest. It was here that King John was absolved by Archbishop Stephen Langton at the termination of their quarrel, and his sentence of excommunication revoked. It was here that Henry III preached to the assembled monks from the text " Righteousness and peace have kissed each other," when he was trying to persuade them to elect his half-brother, Audemar, to the vacant bishopric. Though they knew that Audemar was " destitute of every necessary qualification for the prelacy," the monks, in fear of the King's anger, with " assenting voices but repugnant hearts," acceded to his request, and Audemar became Bishop. It was here again that Henry's son, Prince Edward, knelt to receive the blessing of the Convent before setting out on his Crusade to the Holy Land. The present condition of the Chapter House is due to Bishop Horne, a bigoted reformer, who held the See during Elizabeth's reign, and who surpasses all bishops of every age in the destruction he wrought, both here and at Durham. By his direction the lead was stripped from the roof and sold, and the Chapter House left in its present ruined condition.

The next building on the eastern side of the Cloister was the Calefactory or Warming-House, where a fire was provided in winter at which the Brethren could warm themselves. It is difficult to elucidate the original arrangement of rooms between the transept and the prior's hall, because there is left very little trace and no account of the first storey. But the monks' **Dorter** dormitory or dorter was probably a great rectangular room on the first floor with its longest side running north and south. It probably covered Slype, Chapter House and Calefactory and may even have continued further south as far as the main north wall of the present Deanery. There are certainly traces of a sharp-pitched roof which met the wall of the transept, and the openings which appear to have existed in a wall running east from the Cloister may well have been interior windows for ventilation or lighting and not necessarily exterior ones. The arrangement, at all events, is reasonably well in keeping with Benedictine practice. The communities of this Order built roughly according to a common plan, but varied its details to suit special need or

52

site. The monks' dorter, however, was nearly always on the first floor in line with the transept, sometimes to the north but usually to the south. To attend the night office the religious passed through a door into the transept, descended a stair to ground level and went up into the Choir.

The south-eastern corner of the Cloister was occupied by the Prior's Hall, now part of the Deanery. This is a magnificent building of the middle fifteenth century, and an even older building probably existed on the site. Adjoining this fine Hall and of considerably greater antiquity is the so-called Pilgrims' Cloister, with its four beautiful pointed arches (of which one is unfortunately now built into the house). Here the pilgrims visiting St. Swithun's shrine used to receive broken meat from the Prior's table before leaving the hospitable monastery. For this reason it opened not on to the Cloister proper but on to the outer court, which secular persons were allowed to enter. *Prior's Hall*

The south side of the Cloister was occupied entirely by the refectory or Frater, now completely vanished. It formerly contained the famous Crucifix which, speaking with a human voice, decided the dispute of monks and canons in Aethelwold's day in favour of the former. Of the western range of buildings nothing remains but a singularly beautiful vaulted chamber now used as a dining-room in the house with the verandah porch. Concerning the original purpose of this undercroft there has been considerable dispute. It originally contained no windows, the present ones being modern. This fact alone would seem sufficiently to limit the possibilities of its use, and to render untenable the views that it was once a kitchen or an infirmary, the *Frater* *Cellar* supposition in the latter case being that it had an open loggia on the western side. All that can be said on this point is that it is nothing more than a mere supposition, while the kitchen theory is rendered extremely improbable by the total absence of any trace of a chimney. The most natural supposition from the position of the building is that it was used as a cellar or store-house. Against this the objection has been raised that so fine an apartment would hardly have been built for so mean a purpose. To this may be brought the simple answer, that such was the normal custom of builders in the Middle Ages, as is shown by the comparison of College cellar.

Guest=Hall
To the south of the cloister was no doubt an outer court or Curia, round which were grouped various guest-houses and offices. Of these we have two interesting remains. The first is the late thirteenth century Guest-Hall, now built into the Pilgrims' School. It is a magnificent building with a fine timber roof and handsomely carved hammer-beams. Unfortunately only four of the original five bays survive, but it still remains a vivid and striking testimony to the unstinted hospitality of a great mediaeval monastery. The other relic of the ancient buildings of the Curia is the Priory Stables, which may be seen adjoining Cheyney Court and immediately opposite the Close Gate. Though not themselves in all probability dating back beyond the Restoration period, they doubtless occupy the site of the original stables.

Cheyney Court
Few buildings even in the Close rival both in the interest of their history and in the picturesque-ness of their appearance the old timbers and steep gables of Cheyney Court. In the Middle Ages the Bishop of Winchester was full and

complete ruler under the King of a great part of the city and its environs. The episcopal Soke, or liberty, included the Cathedral precincts, College, St. Cross, and a large part of the land to the south of the town. Over it the Bishop exercised full jurisdiction, and the Mayor had no authority within its bounds. The government of the Soke centred round Cheyney Court. In it the Bishop's bailiff held his court, and twice a year the " Burghmote " was held, when twelve good men and true from the inhabitants of the Soke assembled to assist in the administration of justice and condemned many a ruffian to sit in the Bishop's stocks hard by St. Swithun's Bridge, or to rot in his reeking dungeons beneath the Keep at Wolvesey. Curiously enough this strange constitutional anomaly lasted on into the nineteenth century, and was only brought to an end when the municipal government of the City was reformed in 1835. Cheyney Court is now used as a dwelling-house. In its present form the greater part of it probably dates from the year 1639, which date has been found carved on an oak beam in the hall, but its chief associations are with the Middle Ages.

Of no other monastic buildings have we any trace except for the remains of the Charnel Chapel in the Close wall, just to the west of Cathedral. The burial-ground of the Convent was east of the Cloister, and was approached through the Slype. There was also a garden of herbs, grown for the sake of their medicinal properties, possibly to the west of the Cloister. Some mention should also be made of the Lockbourne, which in two streams drained and purified the monastic buildings. It branched off St. Aethelwold's stream, to which it afterwards returned.   Lastly we must not omit some reference to the wall which enclosed the monastic precincts. It was built originally by King Aethelbald at the request of good Bishop Swithun and saved the Minster from destruction, when the city was captured by the Danes.   It occupied the site of the present Close wall, which is built on its foundations.

Wolvesey Beyond the strong wall which separated the Close of the monks from their Bishop and Abbot (for he was both in one), there rose at this time a formidable castle.   There are sufficient remains to enable us to trace with some certainty the shape and character of the buildings.   Let us take our stand in the tennis court surrounded by the ruins.   We are standing in the centre of

The
Great Hall what was once the Great Hall of the Castle. One can see quite clearly what the length and width of it have been, for the end walls are stand-

See Plan,
p. 12 ing at the north end even to the height of the windows.   This must have been a magnificent place, with its row of windows running round 40 feet from the ground, deeply recessed in the thickness of the Norman wall.   We say Norman advisedly, although, as at St. Cross, the windows begin to be pointed.   Henry de Blois' work was in no way typical of the Early English style, although his masons were feeling their way in that direction.

A daïs stood at the northern end, as an interesting piece of evidence seems to indicate. The string-course (or rim of stone running round the Hall below the windows, like a picture rail) is suddenly and unaccountably raised some feet when it approaches the north end.   This would clearly be desirable, for the sake of symmetry, if a platform or daïs was standing there   On this

56

daïs great scenes must have taken place, for here de Blois arraigned his brother Stephen for his treatment of the Bishops. Here Cardinal Beaufort later on entertained King Henry V on his way to the campaign of Agincourt.

The Hall was shielded by strong defences towards east and south, the two exposed quarters. A great keep stood just east of its centre, and a strong tower stood at the south-east corner. Standing in the cricket field, one can see here the enormous thickness of the Norman walls. Ten feet of solid masonry have actually been added on the outside of a wall already of no mean proportions ; one can trace in the courses of masonry the haste with which the addition was made. One or two interesting points can also be seen. The general weapon of offence was then the battering-ram, and to meet this method of attack, the builders have worked pillars into the masonry (taken, no doubt, from the Conqueror's Palace, which had perished by fire), laying them horizontally in the wall in such a way that their round heads appear on the outside. This device, which was thought greatly to strengthen the wall against the blows of the ram, was probably brought to England by home-coming Crusaders. Finally, on the outside, towards the cricket field, are clear traces of further schemes for dealing with anyone rash enough to approach the walls. Holes and ledges high up mark arrangements for the erection of scaffolds and galleries outside, from which the besieged could conveniently drop upon the heads of the assaulting party boiling oil, melted lead, stones, and so forth. About a foot or two from the ground are mysterious projecting ledges in the masonry, which are connected with the afore-said stones. A stone dropped from the gallery might well fall harmless on the ground below, but if it were dropped in such a way as to bound against a ledge and then ricochet in several pieces in unexpected directions, there was a good chance of execution being done. There was a sally port to the south, and the Chapel probably stood where the present Chapel does at the south-west angle of the Castle-block. (The Bishop's Palace, built later in the seventeenth century, lies outside the area of the old Castle.) The wall of defence ran round the west and north sides as well, though the fortifications were less formidable there than on the east and south. To the north the old gate is still to be seen. It led to the town by a causeway over the marshes which surrounded the whole Castle. The water could be manipulated to great effect on an enemy's approach ; and the whole place had a strong line of outer defence in the city wall which ran round it, so well seen to-day between College and the Weirs.

The third great group of buildings in the town was the Governor's Castle by the West Gate. That will be described in greater length in the next chapter, for it was largely rebuilt at the very end of this period and comes more conveniently under the next heading.

The fourth great group was the Conqueror's Palace in the centre. Of that sufficient account has been given above, since nothing, or almost nothing, remains.

Other Churches The other ecclesiastical buildings we must pass hastily by. Hyde Abbey, built for the monks who left the New Minster in 1110, is now a mere ruined gate.

St. Lawrence's Church, built where the Palace of William had stood, is an interesting Perpendicular church. As a proof of its original connection with the Conqueror, it can still show a Norman door, now kept in a cupboard. St. Maurice's, lower down High Street, can boast a Norman doorway too, and further down on the opposite side is the Chapel of the Knights of St. John. Most interesting of all, but now, unfortunately, completely destroyed, must have been the Hospital of St. Mary Magdalen, that stood at the top of **Magdalen** the hill that bears its name along the road to **Hospital** Alresford, and not far from the modern fever hospital. Lepers were common in those days of dirt and of traffic with the East, and for these poor wretches there was erected about 1180 a most beautiful group of buildings, which must have vaguely resembled St. Cross. It stood till 1788, and then fell, or was pulled down. So we lost a Chapel rivalling in beauty the work of de Blois at St. Cross, and specially interesting as providing a link between that bishop's work and the true Early English of de Lucy. One of its doorways was transferred, and may be seen built into the Roman Catholic Church in St. Peter's Street. To anticipate somewhat, we may add that the Hospital was much thought of by William of Wykeham, who sent his gardener there. It should be said that by then leprosy was almost extinct, and it had become a kind of almshouse for aged and deserving poor. Two other facts connected with it are of special interest. First, Melton, the original headmaster of our own College, was appointed also to be master of the Hospital " as long as he behaved himself well." If the John Melton, who was indicted for stealing from Hursley thirteen pieces of cloth, valued at £7, is the same personage, this would not appear to have been long. Secondly, a better appointment was made in 1430, no less a man than

William of Waynflete, who, rising to be bishop, and desiring to found a College at Oxford, must needs give it the name of St. Mary Magdalen too.

Of the foundation of the Chapel of St. Catharine on St. Catharine's Hill, no record exists, and its history is very meagre. From the remains, a pre-Conquest date can be assigned to the early Chapel, though this was extensively added to, soon after the Conquest. It is first definitely mentioned in historical documents in 1284 and perhaps it is the church of St. Catharine whose belfry was damaged in the great gale of 1268. It was included in the parish of Chilcomb and was finally suppressed by Cardinal Wolsey 1528-9 ; its lease was sold to Thomas Wriothesley, who demolished it. The building was cruciform in shape, divided into three portions built in the Norman style. The earliest part was the east end of the chancel, which was of pre-Conquest date. To this was added *c.* 1110-25 a nave, north and south transepts and an extension of the chancel, which was divided from the earlier building by a wooden screen. Perhaps at the same time, or later, the small building at the north corner of the east end was added. This consisted of a living room and a small ante-room, probably a porch. The quantity of broken cooking pots, domestic utensils and glazed pitchers found there points to a permanent habitation of the building, by a sexton or caretaker, if not a priest, or possibly, as so often in chapels of this sort, by a hermit, who took charge of the building on behalf of the priest of Chilcomb. The whole building was roofed with materials of various colours. The nave and north transept were probably covered with blue slate ; this is a remarkable instance of the mediaeval use of blue slate outside the limits of its geological distribution. Plain and glazed red tiles were found littered about the chancel and south transepts, but whether these were original or put on between the suppression and destruction of the church, when it was in secular hands, it is impossible to say. The domestic rooms seem to have been covered with tiles of yellow and orange glazes and the whole building must have presented a colour-scheme such as can be still found in the glazed-tile roofs of churches in Austria and South Germany. The destruction was so effectively carried out that it is impossible to identify any other buildings or extensions there might have been, and it is extremely difficult to mark the sites even of doors and windows.

The site was excavated between 1925 and 1928 but had to be covered up so as not to interfere with the trees, and all traces of the Chapel are now hidden from view.

The tale of the buildings left to us is now complete. But we cannot do full justice to the great and vigorous ecclesiastical influence in the place during this period without a few more words about monastic life.

Winchester was a stronghold of the Benedictine Order. This Order originated in Italy, where St. Benedict, " the greatest religious personality in European history after the time of St. Paul," issued his famous Rule in 520. The extraordinary wisdom and knowledge of human nature which characterised the injunctions of St. Benedict made certain the rapid spread and permanent importance of his Order : his

Monastic Life

61

regulations were based on four main principles—submission, humility, obedience, and manual labour.

The Order was introduced into England by St. Augustine, who founded the first abbey at Canterbury ; and although as time went on its followers fell into laxer ways, and the newer and stricter Cistercian and Carthusian Orders gained numerous supporters, Benedictinism never entirely lost its hold on the country. To it belonged the three great monastic houses of Winchester : St. Swithun's, the New Minster (by this time moved to Hyde), and the Nuns' Minster. In the thirteenth century fresh rivals appeared in the Mendicant Friars. Each of the four great Orders had a house at Winchester. The Franciscans settled in the Brooks in the north-east corner of the town, where they ministered to the needs of the poor and infirm, a task which the monks proper had never taken up with whole-hearted enthusiasm, though they had always been lavish in doles to the starving and naked. The Friars, however, made " social work " one of the main objects of their existence.

Of the other Orders of Friars, the Carmelites had a house in Meads near the present position of College Sick-house, the Dominicans in the High Street near the Eastgate, and the Austin Friars close to the Southgate, where there is still a house called " the Friary." The possessions of all the four Friars' houses came at the Dissolution to College. The presence of these more popular and more energetic Orders in such large numbers in the town tended somewhat to shake the supremacy of the Benedictines, though the importance of St. Swithun's Monastery was still very considerable. The Prior was one of the great nobles of the kingdom with large estates to manage and plenty of interests outside the narrow limits of conventual routine. This very fact no doubt tended towards the relaxing of discipline and the increase of worldliness within the Convent itself.

Moreover, the brethren soon began to replace the manual labour, which St. Benedict's Rule required and which had done so much to win back barren lands to cultivation, by less strenuous work in the Cloister. This, however, we can hardly regret, since it was by the agency of monastic copyists that many works of classical antiquity were preserved to us, while the monkish chroniclers teach us almost all we can learn about the Middle Ages. The monastery had been from the days of St. Aethelwold a great centre of the illuminator's art. In the scriptorium or writing-room, set apart for the purpose, the brethren devoted themselves to the work of copying books and decorating their copies with the most beautiful miniatures. The magnificent "Benedictional of St. Aethelwold," which rivals in beauty and delicacy of execution even the famous Lindisfarne Gospels, is now in the possession of the Duke of Devonshire. There is still a very fine Vulgate in the Cathedral Library. Histories of secular subjects were also composed, as well as religious treatises ; and one of the brethren even wrote an epic. Mystery plays were also performed from time to time, and the artistic skill of the community, which was not expended in the illuminating of books, was devoted to the painting of frescoes in the north transept of the Cathedral and the Chapel of the Castle. These occupations, innocent though they were, still marked a decline from the earlier austerity of the Order ; but in spite of all, life was strict enough, and the inconveniences considerably greater than most of us moderns would willingly endure. Let us examine the daily time-table of a great Monastic House.

Matins

A great part of the day was devoted to services in the Church. The earliest of these began at midnight, when the sacristan, who slept near the Church, arose, lit the lights on the stairs from the Dormitory, and also in the Church. Meanwhile the brethren in the Dormitory itself, having been awakened by the Prior, rose from their beds, put on their fur-lined night boots, and descended into the church, preceded by a junior monk carrying a light. The superior remained behind until all the Convent were in their places, and then, having given the signal for the tolling of the bell to cease, entered the Choir, whereupon all rose and bowed to him. This ceremony over, the service began with the chanting of the " Triple-Prayer "—the Pater, Ave, and Creed. Then followed the fifteen " gradual psalms " (CXX to CXXXIV). After this the bell rang again, and any officials having special duties to perform were permitted to leave the Choir. Next followed Matins proper, which consisted of various antiphons, psalms and lessons. An official named the " Circa " patrolled meanwhile with a lantern, which, on finding a brother asleep, he would deposit under his nose. The culprit, waking with a start, fell on his knees, begged for pardon, and then, taking up the lantern himself, continued the perambulation of the Choir until he found another victim of drowsiness.

The singing throughout was directed by the Cantor or Precentor, who was selected for his musical ability. He had also to find the places

64

in the book of the lessons, and point out to the reader where he was to begin. If the Prior was to read the lesson, as happened on great feasts, the Cantor, together with his assistants and the Prior's Chaplain, brought the book to his stall and stood close at hand to assist him with the chanting. The Cantor was also directed to supervise the behaviour of the choir-boys ; for " if he found the boys fibbing or novices careless in the Choir," he was bidden " tweak the boys' ears, pull out their hair, or smite them with the fist."

When Matins was over the bell rang for the next service. During the interval the monks were allowed to walk in the Cloister in order to restore the circulation to their chilled limbs. When the bell stopped, Lauds or the " Praise **Lauds** song of the Dawn " began. The Cantor had previously marked the places in the great chained Antiphonary or Anthem Book, and when the various anthems had been sung, the brethren filed out of the Choir and back to the Dormitory for another five hours' sleep before Prime, the sacristan remaining behind to see that all the lights were extinguished and the books returned to their aumbry or cupboard, before he, too, withdrew to his bed in a room near the church. The time would now be about half-past one. At seven o'clock the bell was again ringing for Prime, which was followed by the early Mass, mainly intended for the servants of the establishment. The brethren were not bound to attend this service, and withdrew to wash in the lavatory in the Cloister, where there was a cupboard containing towels. The priests had the first use of the lavatory, as they had to say their private Masses, and later the juniors and novices took their turn. Some of the monks at this time withdrew to the Chapter-House, where they would be certain of finding a confessor.

Morning Mass

Before the next service, the Morning or Chapter Mass, the community repaired to the refectory, where they partook of a slender meal, called the Mixtum, consisting of a quarter of a pound of bread, and a third of a pint of wine or beer. Even this was denied them in Lent and on days of fasting. After this the brethren assembled at about 8.30 and walked in procession into the church for the Morning Mass. This was also sometimes called the Lady Mass, being celebrated in the Lady Chapel. From the Mass the monks

Chapter Meeting

proceeded to the Chapter House, where faults were corrected (flogging being the usual form of punishment imposed), and questions concerning the whole house were considered. This was followed by the Parliament or consultation (whence the political use of the term) at which the various officials of the monastery discussed the affairs of their offices, and the transactions necessary to the administration of a great establishment were carried on. Meanwhile in another part of the Cloister the rest of the brethren devoted themselves to reading and meditation, and the novice-master to the instruction of his pupils.

High Mass

High Mass was celebrated at ten o'clock. At this service the Prior and senior monks occupied the stalls nearest the Altar, instead of those at the west end of the choir, their places on other occasions. The Mass was sung by the " Hebdomadarian " or priest on duty for the week. On Sunday the service began with the blessing of the salt for the refectory tables and also the holy water, with which the priest then sprinkled the altar, and all the religious in the choir. Then

66

followed the procession round the cloister. On one occasion, having a difference of opinion with their bishop, the brethren went in procession round the triforium with crosses reversed, head downwards, and dismal chantings and—unheard-of impropriety—in a direction against the sun. This form of protest proved eminently successful, as the bishop hasted to be reconciled with the Convent, and lived in peace and amity with them for the rest of his days.

Mass being finished dinner followed, usually **Dinner** at about eleven o'clock. The Prior, or in his absence, one of the senior monks, presided, sitting at the high table. The rest of the brethren when they entered were directed to bow to the Crucifix at the end of the Hall, and remain standing until the president had taken his place. As he walked up the Hall each monk bowed to him, and he returned the salutation. When all was ready he rang a small bell, and the monk appointed to read having mounted the pulpit * in the wall, pronounced the first sentence, and then the president rang his bell a second time as a sign that the meal might begin. The passage to be read during the meal was usually taken from some pious book, and it is no doubt a survival of this custom that a passage from the Gospel is still read at Domum Dinner by the Prefect of Hall.

Some samples of the menu, together with the **Menu** prices of the day, may be of interest. On the 29th of November, 1492, the monks' dinner consisted of drylynge (dried ling or cod), 3s. 11d. ; mushrooms, 3s. 4d. ; oysters as entrée, 4d. ; mustard, 1½d.

* The present parish church of Beaulieu, which is the old monastic refectory, contains a fine pulpit of this type.

On Christmas Day of the same year the menu, as befitted the occasion, was more elaborate—spiced vegetables, 4*d*. ; moile (bread held under the cooking meat so as to catch the dripping), 7*d*. ; 210 eggs, 1*s*. 8*d*. ; nombles (the inner parts of venison, regarded as a special delicacy), 2*d*. ; burson (bread and dripping) for pittance, granted to monks who had performed special duties, 4*d*. ; sew (onion broth), 8*d*. ; beef, 3*s*. 4*d*. ; mutton, 1*s*. 11*d*. ; extra for the sub-Prior and Hordarian, one of the officials connected with the catering, 6*d*. ; wine to the Lord Prior, 1*s*. 3*d*. For Good Friday, 1493—1000 eggs, 3*s*. 4*d*. ; red herrings, 5*s*. ; figs as entrée, 8*d*.

The reader and those who had served at the first dinner had their meal afterwards, and when they had finished the whole community repaired to the church for None. This service over, the brethren were more or less free until Vespers at 6 o'clock in summer, and 5 in winter. During the summer months they took an hour's siesta in the middle of the day. The rest of the afternoon was spent in various ways ; the juniors and novices were allowed to play games or stroll in the Convent garden. These recreations were even sometimes permitted in the Cloister, for at Canterbury, Westminster and Gloucester traces may be seen of the holes and squares drawn for this purpose on the pavement. Nor were some of the elder monks above a little amusement. Numerous strange pets such as apes, peacocks, cranes, falcons, and bears were kept by the community and fed daily by the cellarer. Others of a more serious bent devoted their leisure time to reading or copying in the scriptorium. While the western walk of the Cloister was set apart for the juniors, the northern, and therefore sunny side nearest the church, was devoted to the use of the senior monks. Each had his special place, the Prior's being at the east end nearest the church door. The part of the walk nearest the garth was, as a rule, divided by wooden wainscotting into little divisions, known as " carrels," containing a desk on which to rest books. (It is possible that these carrels were the originals from which our own Toys were imitated.) There was a large selection of edifying works which might be borrowed from the Library. Among them were Bede's *Ecclesiastical History, Cassiodorus on the Psalms, The Origin and Education of Judas Iscariot,* and *The History of the Early Life of Pontius Pilate.* Once a year the Cantor, who also acted as librarian, called in the books and examined their condition. Some of the monks were also occupied in teaching the boys at the High School in Symonds' Street, which was perhaps the germ of our own foundation. Others again might be entertained by the Prior, who was allowed to ask a few of the seniors to drink a glass of wine with him from time to time and warm themselves at his fire. Agriculture was, as we have said, out of favour among St. Swithun's monks ; and one of the brethren so much regretted that fact that he left the Benedictine for the more austere Carthusian Order. He seems, however, on second thoughts, to have returned.

At five o'clock in winter and six in summer the bell rang for Vespers, which was followed by supper in the refectory, the ceremonial being similar to that at dinner. In Advent, Lent, and at other seasons, when there was no supper, those of the monks who so desired might obtain a drink and a small portion of bread at the refectory. After this had been eaten they all assembled in the Chapter House for the reading called Collation. This did not last long, and the interval between it and Compline was spent in walking in the Cloister, or during the winter months in warming at the fire in the Calefactory. Here, on special occasions, they made merry with " Figs, raisins, ale, and cakes : and of these no superfluity or excess, but a scholastical and moderate congratulation among themselves." At seven they collected for the last time in the church for the singing of Compline. As soon as the service was over, the brethren arose and left the church, being sprinkled with holy water as they passed out of the door. Thus by about half-past seven, or in summer an hour later, the whole community were in bed, snatching the three or four hours' sleep allowed them, before they rose for the midnight office of next day.

No account of monastic life would be complete without some reference to the hospitality which the great houses so freely dispensed to travellers and pilgrims. When a visitor appeared at the gate, a message was at once sent to the Guest Master, who was bidden to receive all strangers " as Christ Himself." The Guest Master conducted the traveller first to the church, where he was sprinkled with holy water, and then took him to the Pilgrims' Hall. Here he enquired the stranger's name and if he was of inferior degree, prepared a bed for him and made him as comfortable as possible. If the guest proved to be some great person, the Guest Master informed the Prior, who received and entertained him in his Hall. The monastery undertook to provide for all wayfarers and pilgrims for two days. This gave them plenty of time to pay

The Guest Master

their devotions at St. Swithun's shrine and the various other altars of the church. When they departed, the Guest Master was bidden to send them on their way, having previously taken the precaution to see that they had left nothing behind and had also taken nothing away. Thus many a pilgrim left St. Swithun's hospitable roof and set out rejoicing for Farnham, and thence by Guildford and Dorking and the old Pilgrims' Way to the shrine of St. Thomas at Canterbury.

The Later Mediaeval Period

WHEN Earl Simon fell at Evesham his work was really completed, for he had given England a heritage of which she has never lost hold—the heritage of Parliamentary Government. When Edward I called his first Parliament, in imitation of Simon's " House of Commons," he held it up at the Great Hall in the Castle of Winchester.

Winchester Retires from Public Life With that illustrious event the public history of Winchester practically closes. The court is shifted to Westminster : and our city ceases to be the seat of kings, or the meeting-place of Parliaments. Perhaps we have much to be thankful for.

Its Bishops Henceforward the happiness or unhappiness of the town depended almost entirely upon the character of a single man, the Bishop. He was now sole monarch of his little kingdom : and through the fourteenth and fifteenth centuries many notable and strong men sat in the chair of St. Swithun. It was " the wealthiest See in the land " : and so it was that " low-minded kings gave it to their favourites and the nobler monarchs to their ministers." And it came to pass that the Bishop of Winchester often held the Chancellorship of the realm, and when the Order of the Garter was established, he became its Prelate.

Pontoise John of Pontoise held the See during most of Edward the First's reign. He was popularly known as Sawbridge, a pun based upon a false derivation of his name, Pontissera, the Latin for Pontoise. He ruled Winchester well, and founded the College of St. Elizabeth for the propagation

72

of learning and piety. It stood in the present Warden's garden, and shall be dealt with hereafter. His monument is in the Choir of the Cathedral, partly let into Fox's screen, under the coffer of King Egbert.

After Edward the Second had succeeded to the throne, the first bishop of importance was John of Stratford. He had been Edward's **John of** Chancellor, and, much to the King's annoyance, **Stratford** though at the wish of the Pope, deserted that office for the bishopric. He took no very creditable part in the disgusting story of plotting and treachery that brought Edward's reign to a close. He joined himself, in fact, to that conspiracy of the Queen and Mortimer, which dethroned the wretched half-imbecile king. The Earl of Winchester on the other hand, Hugh the Dispenser, an old man of 90, played a truer part ; he stood by the king, but was taken at Bristol after a gallant defence, hung, as he was, in his armour, and his body cut up and thrown to the dogs, while his head was sent to Winchester as a warning to the inhabitants. After this, one does not sympathise much with our Bishop, when he fell under Mortimer's displeasure. He was forced to fly from the town, and was hunted like a wild beast from place to place, living now at Wilton Abbey, and now in Waltham Chase. However, he lived to see Mortimer's fall, and rose to be Archbishop of Canterbury.

We have now arrived at the end of the first third of the fourteenth century—a century which is marked in the history of the town by the two great names of Edyngton and Wykeham. The worst of civil strife was over, and even during the subsequent Wars of the Roses Winchester seems to repose in a backwater. Nevertheless

73

she had to undergo about the middle of this fourteenth century two severe trials which left her partially crippled. Little reference has been made hitherto to her manufactures. It was about this time that she took the lead in the wool industry of the south. In 1333 Edward III, for the convenience of foreigners, appointed this town, as far as we can discover, to be the central wool-mart of England. St. Giles' Fair was a great gathering-place for representatives of all nations, and a market for all goods from the East brought by Venetians and Genoese. The monks were not backward in taking advantage of this commerce, while the main control of the Fair lay in the Bishop's hands. Probably we may date from this time the chains and hooks used for weighing wool, which are still preserved in the West Gate Museum. In the midst of this prosperity the two blows fell. In 1338 Southampton was destroyed by the French, and Winchester was thus deprived of her port. Ten years later, just when the country was still ringing with the triumph of Crecy, came an even severer trial. The Black Death swept raging through England. It dealt a final and crushing blow to the wool trade, besides filling the countryside with discontented workmen, who readily took advantage of the scarcity of labour to go on strike. As for Winchester, the King removed his wool staple to Calais in 1363, and soon after we read how 1000 houses stood empty here, and seventeen churches fell to decay.

But the lower her fortunes sank, the more remarkable and illustrious were her Bishops. In 1345 William of Edyngton, King's Treasurer, and a constant favourite of Edward (for it was he that became Prelate of the new Order

74

of the Garter), was appointed to the See of Winchester.

To him belongs the credit of introducing the new style of architecture into the Cathedral. He pulled down the old Norman west front and built the present one, thus cutting the Nave shorter by some 40 feet. The new style was called Perpendicular—a peculiar product of the English genius, which seems to have grown up almost as a protest against that misuse of stonework on the Continent that goes by the name of Flamboyant. While the French were twisting and torturing the tracery of their windows into unimaginable branchings, the sober English Bishop contented See Plate in Appendix himself with straight, vertical shafts, severe even to a fault, and, to say the least of it, uninspired, as if the Black Death had taken the heart out of the builders. No doubt Edyngton meant well, but it is better not to think too much about the grand Norman towers that have vanished when one looks at our present west end. He also began work on the north-west corner of the Nave, which he transformed in a similar way ; it was left for a more skilful hand to continue his work. Meanwhile, in 1366, he was offered the archbishopric. He persisted for some time in his refusal—in all humility : though one venomous author ascribes to him the saying, " Canterbury is the higher rack, but Winchester the richer manger." But as a matter of fact he was too old for such an elevation, and in the same year he died, and was buried in the Cathedral, where his chapel is still to be seen. But we have better cause still to be grateful to Edyngton. It was he that discovered William of Wykeham.

Wykeham

The latter was born at Wickham (or as it was then spelt, Wykeham), a village in the Meon

75

Valley about thirteen miles from Winchester. The date of his birth is uncertain, but it was somewhere between July 8th and September 27th, 1324. His father was John Longe, a yeoman of the district, but his mother was of gentle birth. They were poor and William was sent to a grammar school at Winchester (which stood at the corner of Minster and Symonds Streets) by Sir John Scures, lord of the manor of Wickham and constable of Winchester Castle. On leaving school he did not go up to Oxford but became Sir John's secretary, and afterwards held the same post under Bishop Edyngton. At this time Wykeham used regularly to attend the Mass, which was celebrated daily in the nave of the Cathedral.

His appointment in Bishop Edyngton's household was destined to lead him even higher. In 1347 King Edward III passed through Winchester on his way home after the taking of Calais and was entertained by the Bishop at Wolvesey. Edyngton recommended his secretary to the King, who accordingly took him into his service.

After holding various minor offices, he was in 1356 appointed Surveyor of Windsor Forest and Chief Warden and Surveyor of the royal castles of Windsor, Leeds, Dover and Hadleigh. He superintended the erection of the new additions to Windsor Castle and the building of the Castle of Queenborough in the Isle of Sheppey. The tradition, which makes him the actual architect either of these or of his later buildings, has been questioned, and it is suggested that William Winford, whom he employed as master-mason, acted also as architect.

In 1364 Wykeham was promoted to be keeper of the Privy Seal, and in the following year was appointed one of the commissioners to arrange a peace with Scotland. So great was his influence over the King at this time that, as Froissart tells us, " everything was done through him, and without him was nothing done." In consideration of his " excessive labours and expenses " in the King's service he was granted an extra allowance of a pound a day.

A return of the Black Death in 1361 brought him a veritable shower of prebends and other rich benefices, with a result that he at last decided to take Orders, and was ordained acolyte in December, 1361, and priest the following June.

In 1366 died Wykeham's old patron, Bishop **Elected** Edyngton ; and on the King's recommendation **Bishop** the monks of St. Swithun unanimously elected Wykeham to the vacant bishopric. But the Pope had, according to the custom of the time, " reserved " to himself the right of appointing to the see, and refused to confirm the election of Wykeham, though he invested him with the administration of the spirituals and temporals of the see. After prolonged negotiations, carried on through the mediation of the Duke of Bourbon, one of the hostages of the Treaty of Brétigny, Urban V at length consented to solve the difficulty by himself " providing " Wykeham to the bishopric. He was accordingly consecrated in St. Paul's on October 10th, 1367, and enthroned at Winchester on July 8th, 1368.

Shortly after he was firmly established in the **First** bishopric, the King appointed him to succeed **Chancellor=** Archbishop Langham as Chancellor. The office **ship** of Chancellor was at that time by far the greatest in the kingdom, and conferred on its holder the real direction of the policy of the country. Wykeham's tenure of the office was not a very successful one. He succeeded to the leadership of the government at a time when the early glories of Edward's reign were already passed, and the war in France was draining to their utmost limits the resources of the country without any adequate return. The loss of Ponthieu, coming after a series of unsuccessful campaigns, served as a sufficient excuse for a change of administration, and the opposition, led by the Earl of Pembroke, succeeded in bringing about the fall of Wykeham in 1371.

His
Reforms

The Bishop now turned his attention to the affairs of his diocese, where he set himself to correct abuses. He incurred the hostility of the monks of St. Swithun by an attempt to reform their lax discipline, while the vigorous measures which he adopted against two corrupt and unscrupulous Masters of St. Cross, who had appropriated the funds of the Hospital to their own use, involved him in protracted litigation in the Papal Court. It was only after the proceedings had dragged on for six years that the verdict was finally pronounced in Wykeham's favour, and he was able to hand over the administration of the Hospital to his kinsman, Nicholas Wykeham.

It was at this period that he first made preparations for founding two Colleges for poor scholars, one at Oxford and the other at Winchester. His object was to bring into being a body of educated clerks, from whom might be replenished the ranks of the secular clergy, sorely depleted by the Black Death. As early as 1369 he had begun buying land for this purpose at Oxford, and in 1376 seventy scholars were lodged at his expense in various halls on the site now occupied by the cloisters of New College. Three years earlier he had engaged one Richard Herton

to instruct seventy poor students at Winchester
"in arte grammatica." He eventually converted
this school into his College by making it permanent and granting it a charter of incorporation,
which enabled it to hold land, manors and benefices.

His plans in this direction were unfortunately **Quarrel with**
interrupted in 1376. John of Gaunt and the **John of**
party which had succeeded Wykeham in power **Gaunt and**
in 1371 had been equally unsuccessful, and in **Disgrace**
the Good Parliament Wykeham led the attack
upon them. His alliance with the Commons and
his friendship with the Black Prince (who at his
death nominated him one of his executors) made
him a formidable opponent, and he succeeded in
bringing about the fall of Lord Latimer, one of
John of Gaunt's supporters. On the dissolution
of the Good Parliament, however, the Duke
avenged himself upon the Bishop. Wykeham
was accused of misgovernment and malversation
of the public revenue during the period of his
Chancellorship. He appeared before the Council
"well accompanyed, but with a pensive
countenance, and with him ye bishop of London
to comfort him, and some sixe serjeantes of the
lawe of his counsaile." But neither these allies
nor the generally fictitious character of the charges
brought against him served to protect him from
the sentence of an enormous fine of nearly a
million marks. John of Gaunt at a subsequent
sitting of the Council brought further charges
against him, but his brother bishops claimed
immunity for his "parsone and spiritualtyes,"
and the Council could do no more than confiscate
his temporalities and order him to appear again
before them on January 20th. The huge fine was
a sufficiently serious penalty, for it compelled him

79

to break up his household and send word to his Oxford scholars to return to their homes. Being forbidden to appear within twenty miles of the Court, he lived in retirement in various monastic houses in his diocese. His trial was further postponed, but in February Convocation espoused his cause and the Londoners demanded his trial by his peers. John of Gaunt replied by granting Wykeham's temporalities to the young Richard, son of the Black Prince and afterwards Richard II, hoping in this way to split up the party which supported Wykeham. When, on the occasion of Edward III's jubilee, a general pardon was issued, Wykeham was specially excepted from it. " By no means," ran the proclamation, " is it the King's wish that Sir William of Wykeham, Bishop of Winchester, shall be comprehended within the pardon and grace aforesaid, or enjoy anything of them." At last, three days before the old King's death, Wykeham's temporalities were restored to him on condition that he fitted out three ships and maintained them for three months against the French invasion, which was then expected. With the accession of Richard II, Wykeham's troubles came to an end. He received a pardon and was declared guiltless in respect of the charges alleged against him. He attended the new King's coronation and was afterwards reconciled by him with the Duke of Lancaster.

His Foundations As soon as he was once again in possession of the revenues of his see, Wykeham resumed the educational projects, which had been interrupted by his disgrace. In 1379 he issued the charter of foundation of the " Seinte Marie College of Wynchestre in Oxenforde." The first stone was laid in March, 1380, and on April 14th, 1386, the warden and scholars took possession of the

80

finished buildings "cum cruce erecta et litania
sollemniter cantata." At the same time Wykeham
began the building of his other foundation, the
"Seinte Marie College of Wynchestre." He
obtained a Papal Bull for the endowment of the
College in 1378, and issued his charter of foundation four years later. The actual building was
begun the year after the opening of New College,
and was completed in 1394. Eight months after
the entry of the warden and scholars into College,
Wykeham began rebuilding the Norman Nave of
the Cathedral. He seems first to have contemplated
a continuation of Edyngton's alterations in 1371,
when we are told that he undertook a "new
work" in Cathedral ; but these operations were
interrupted, probably owing to his quarrel with
the monks.

During these years Wykeham was still playing
a leading part in politics. In 1386 he was
appointed a member of the Council of Regency,
but he does not seem to have taken a very active
part in their proceedings. At any rate he, unlike
most of his colleagues, did not incur the wrath
and hatred of the young king. On the contrary,
when the latter, in 1389, suddenly declared
himself of age, he wisely chose Wykeham as his
Chancellor. Wykeham owed much to young **Second**
Richard, and there is a curious token of his **Chancellor=**
gratitude in the line of bosses that runs along **ship**
beneath the triforium of the Nave. Many of these
bear Richard's emblem, a stag couchant chained
to an oak. One may remark also the portrait of
Richard on the corbel outside the east end of
College Chapel. The aged bishop reluctantly
accepted the office, which he resigned after two
years, thinking that he had established the
King's government on a firm basis. From

this time onward he took little part in public life.

In 1392 he signed his will, in which he expressed the wish to be buried in the Nave of the Cathedral at the spot where, as a lad, he had been wont to attend Mass, and there shortly before his death he endowed a chantry. He also bequeathed his crozier to New College and his bible to Winchester. At last his health broke down, and in 1401 he was unable to administer ordination. He retired to South (now Bishop's) Waltham, only a few miles from his birth-place at Wickham.

Death

During the year 1404 his strength gradually failed, and at last, on September 27th, he passed away. He was buried, as he desired, in the chapel he had built in the Cathedral. The effigy on his tomb is said to be a good likeness, but probably the best in existence is on one of the corbels in College muniment room, which was made some ten or twelve years before his death.

Character

Such, then, is the remarkable story of a poor yeoman's son. Possibly, as Dean Kitchin says, he had " no genius or originality about him " ; but he was an able administrator, a reforming bishop, a splendid builder, a great patron of learning and a kind and generous man. His efforts to reform St. Cross prove him to have been honestly desirous to correct abuses. His two great foundations show that he understood well the educational needs of his time. But nothing is more remarkable or more typical of the man than his extraordinary generosity. Not only did he rebuild the nave of the Cathedral and endow with unheard-of munificence his two Colleges, but his consideration for the poor and suffering showed itself in many less known acts of charity. One of his first acts on his appointment to the See of Winchester was to excuse his poorer tenants of rent to the extent of £500 ; on three separate occasions he paid out of his own purse his tenants' share of a subsidy voted by Parliament ; twenty-four poor men fed daily at his table, and he kept open house to rich and poor alike. Certainly he did much good to Winchester, not least in that he gave it its School.

His successor was a man of a very different type, no poor man's son, but born in the purple, son of John of Gaunt and half-brother of the usurper Henry IV. Beaufort had bad blood in **Beaufort** him that did not fail to show, and if he did not entirely earn the name of the " bad Cardinal," he was at least a selfish, worldly man, and never a serious Churchman. As a youth, he had studied law at Oxford, Cambridge, and Aix in France. He had been thrust irregularly into the See of Lincoln, and was transferred to Winchester on Wykeham's death, receiving soon after the Cardinal's scarlet hat. He was the friend and tutor of young Prince Hal, who was educated at New College in Oxford. But it is typical of the worldly-wise Cardinal, that, when Sir John Oldcastle, Shakespeare's Falstaff, was condemned as a Lollard, he did not stir a finger for the Prince's friend.

He took no small part in the stirring events abroad. The fat purse of this princely bishop was, no doubt, useful to King Henry V in his French campaigns, and Beaufort gave him a fine send-off on the expedition that ended in Agincourt. When the child king Henry VI succeeded to the throne, the Cardinal went with the Regent to France, and took part in the trial and execution of Jeanne d'Arc. He engineered the King's marriage with Margaret of Anjou,

and died three years after. " Lord Cardinal,"
says the *King* in Shakespeare's play,

> "If thou think'st on heaven's bliss,
> Hold up thy hand, make signal of thy hope.
> He dies and makes no sign. O God, forgive him."

At any rate he conferred some benefits on
Winchester ; he added to de Blois' foundation
at St. Cross the Hospital of Noble Poverty,
intended as a refuge for decayed noblemen,
victims of the changes and chances of the fifteenth
century troubles, and of the breaking up of
Feudalism. He finished Wykeham's work in
Cathedral, repaired Hyde Abbey, and built himself a chapel in the Cathedral, where his body
now lies.

Henry VI liked Winchester, and above all
liked the School. He even gave it " his best
robe but one, lined in sable " : he also gave it
Waynflete a notable bishop. One William Patten was
Headmaster of the College : when Eton, Henry's
new foundation, was ready, Patten was elevated
to the dignity of Provost there, but on Beaufort's
death became Bishop of Winchester with the
sounding title of William of Waynflete.

This able statesman was already a supporter of
the House of Lancaster, but in those disastrous
years that followed, when England was convulsed
from end to end with the ceaseless struggle of
Wars of the Roses, he managed things with such con-
the Roses summate skill that he avoided giving offence to
either side, and kept himself and his city absolutely
free from the tumult of war.

Kings begin to pass in rapid succession across
the scene, and, compared with the long-lived trio
—Wykeham, Beaufort, and Waynflete—whose
bishoprics covered between them 120 years,
the Bishops pass rapidly, too : Courtenay, who

witnessed the addition of the late Perpendicular Lady Chapel at the extreme east end : Langton, who died of the plague in 1500 : and Richard Fox, Fox and others who completed the great screen of Cathedral, the clerestory, and the roof of the choir, besides building his own exquisite chapel. Fox was a leading statesman, and while he was blind and dying at Wolvesey, another and a greater man was watching eagerly for his decease. In 1528 Wolsey became Bishop—but he never came to the town—and two years later he made way for the last of the statesmen-bishops, Gardiner. The Reformation had arrived. Its story must be told in another place, but meanwhile a word or two in conclusion on Winchester. An important incident had occurred here in 1491—no less an event than the birth of Henry VII's eldest son at Birth of Prince Arthur the Castle. Henry, who was something of a poseur, called him Arthur in memory of Winchester's mythical hero : and he followed this up by confirming an ancient privilege of the town, namely, the keeping of a standard set of weights and measures. He presented the town with several new measures, of which the bushel (still to be seen at the Westgate) was the most famous.

When Walkelin first built his Norman Minster, Transforma= tion of the Cathedral it seemed solid enough to last for ever. But his Norman masonry was not so substantial as it seemed, and it is probable that the west end was in bad condition by the time of Bishop Edyngton (1345—1366) who set his hand to change it. He was doubtless also swayed by the lust for rebuilding which characterised so many mediaeval bishops. When he pulled down the west front West Front he rebuilt it in the new Perpendicular style—then just developed in England—whose principal features are simplicity, repetition of straight lines

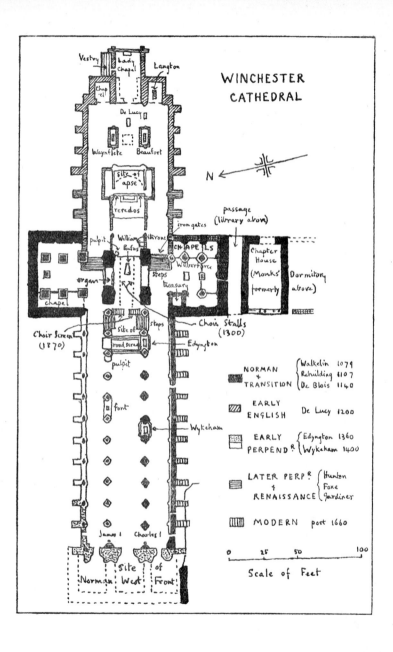

WINCHESTER CATHEDRAL

N

Vestry
Lady Chapel
Langton
Chap-el
De Lucy
Waynflete
Beaufort
site of apse
reredos

passage (library above)

pulpit
William Rufus
Throne
iron gates
CHAPELS
Wilberforce
Chapter House (Monks' formerly)
Dormitory above)
organ
Steps
treasury
chapel
Choir Stalls (1300)
Choir Screen (1870)
site of rood screen
steps
pulpit
Edyngton
font
Wykeham
James I
Charles I
Site of
Norman West
of Front

NORMAN & TRANSITION — Walkelin 1079, Rebuilding 1107, De Blois 1140

EARLY ENGLISH — De Lucy 1200

EARLY PERPEND.ʳ — Edyngton 1360, Wykeham 1400

LATER PERP.ʳ & RENAISSANCE — Hunton, Foxe, Gardiner

MODERN post 1660

0   25   50   100
Scale of Feet

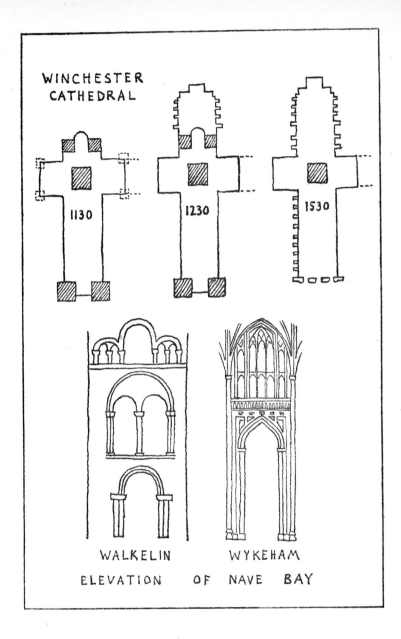

WINCHESTER CATHEDRAL

1130

1230

1530

WALKELIN   WYKEHAM

ELEVATION   OF   NAVE   BAY

both perpendicular and horizontal, and the stone-panelling which gives variety and relief to the blank spaces of the wall. In this style he built the west window, which now seems large and rather vacant, but was obviously finer with its original glass. The window in the gable above is probably Wykeham's work, and the evidence is interesting. Whenever we find Wykeham's work, the cusps (or points in the heads of the windows) are quite plain, whereas Edyngton's end in a little strawberry leaf. The cusps of the window in question are plain. Edyngton took the west end back about 40 feet from Walkelin's front, and pulled down the two towers: the stone was perhaps used for paving Kingsgate Street. He also meant to rebuild the nave, but he only completed the first two bays on the north. The two windows and the two buttresses on the north side of the nave and next the west end are **Edyngton's Work** clearly of quite a different class of workman-ship from the rest of the Cathedral. Among other differences, Edyngton's buttresses have four "sets-off" or projecting ledges, Wykeham's only three. Here Edyngton's work ceased: this is probably very lucky, as he was not an able builder. His west front is one of the least fortunate pieces of work in the Cathedral, while Wykeham's nave is one of the finest. It is remarkable that Edyngton's front is not bonded on in any way, but merely leans against the stump of the Norman nave within with nothing but gravity and a thin layer of mortar to keep it in position.

Wykeham's Work Here Edyngton's work stopped. We cannot say in what state he left the church, but the work obviously had to be continued. This was done by his successor, William of Wykeham (1366—1404), who took up the task right at the end of his life, after he had made his two celebrated foundations. Wykeham had had considerable experience in building, and his method differed from Edyngton's. For, whereas Edyngton pulled down, and then rebuilt from the ground, Wykeham transformed the masonry as it stood. The eight west columns on the south side are the original Norman work re-cut by Wykeham. He may have done it by taking the pillars down stone by stone, re-cutting them, and putting them back again. The broad joints characteristic of the Norman mortar may still be seen. But after that, finding perhaps that this sort of pillar was insecure, he changed his method, and all the pillars on the north side have been re-faced with stone from Quarr in the Isle of Wight ; the core, however, is still Norman, and here and there an older stone peeps out. The last two pillars on the south side have been re-centred with steel in the last century.

His reconstruction of the Nave is hard to understand without a diagram. Looking up from the ground, the Norman nave consisted—as the transepts still do—of three tiers, arches, triforium and clerestory. Of these the triforium has disappeared, leaving only galleries, not a continued passage. The arches are much taller and cut right into what was the Norman triforium, reaching about where the capitals of the pillars would have been. Then after a small balcony comes the clerestory, so that there are two nearly equal compartments instead of three. This results in a large gain in the effect of height obtained. The wall space between the balcony and the springing of the primitive fan vaulting is panelled all over in the " Perpendicular " manner invented at Gloucester but only the central compartments are pierced and glazed.

The Nave

See Figures p. 87

Then to crown his work, Wykeham replaced the Norman wooden roof with a splendid stone vault. Its weight is enormous, and to meet the strain and resist the outward thrust, Wykeham adopted flying buttresses. These may be seen beneath the aisle roof, and consist of a stone prop carried outwards and downwards over the aisles from where the vault rests on the pillars of the nave. In this way the thrust was carried out to the outer walls of the aisles. Unluckily insufficient steps were taken to receive this pressure. Although buttresses were built along the north side, their foundations were so badly built that they did no good, and had to be re-laid. On the south side Wykeham did not strengthen the Norman wall at all. The builders of Durham Cathedral and of the great Abbey churches at Caen used no buttresses, but made their piers and walls thick enough to carry a stone vault by brute strength alone. This, too, may have been projected by the builders of Winchester, Peterborough and Ely, in which case Wykeham's vaulting is less a daring architectural feat than a belated completion of an original scheme, executed in the fashion of the times. The Cloisters, of course, were built close up against the wall of the south aisle of the nave. A Gothic Cloister probably replaced a humbler Norman structure and may have been designed to support the wall behind as far as possible. In 1912, when the foundations of the whole building were renewed, a row of free standing buttresses was placed beside the south aisle wall. The thrust of the nave vault, which Wykeham transferred to the aisle wall by means of stone struts under the roof, is now in large part carried a stage further by means of a second set of flying buttresses to these external free uprights of stone. This is the true Gothic principle. Although these twentieth century additions are structurally sound in design, aesthetically they are abominable. To realise this it is only necessary to walk round to the north side of the nave where Wykeham's buttresses (though before the restoration they were doing more harm than good) look very fine and beautiful.

The vault in every sense sets the coping stone on Wykeham's work. To it more than to any other feature does the Nave owe its magnificence. But it is also helped by the size of the pillars, which are larger than most Perpendicular ones owing to their Norman core. Beneath them runs a solid strip of masonry stretching from beyond the west front to the reredos—Walkelin's Norman foundations. It is interesting to note that the builders of the choir end, behind the reredos, failed to calculate aright. A few moments' inspection, standing between Fox's and Gardiner's chapels, will reveal the fact that the two walls are not set at the same angle to a line drawn straight down the middle of the church.

There is, however, one considerable problem in connection with Wykeham's work in the church, and that is how much of the work was actually completed in his lifetime—that is between 1394 and 1404. There are two clues. One is his Will, in which he leaves instructions that the windows shall be glazed in the aisles north and south and in the south clerestory of the nave. This implies that the north clerestory was not ready for glazing : but that the southern pillars of the nave and both outer walls were. The second clue lies in the treatment of the great bosses under the balconies all along the nave. Over the eight pillars that are merely Norman

Position at Wykeham's Death

masonry re-cut the bosses are small and meagre. Over the pillars that have been re-cased—*i.e.*, the three most easterly of the south, and all the north side—the bosses are rich and massive. This looks like some change in the plan of the architect : or does it mark the point where Wykeham's death occurred ? Is the second type of pillar the work of his executors ? Against this theory there is one fact. Among the bosses on the north side is the white hart couchant of Richard II. This can hardly have been put there in open defiance of Henry IV after Richard's deposition in 1399 : yet Wykeham owed much to Richard and may well have wished to commemorate him in his own work. Moreover, Henry IV must have had more important things to do than to go round every cathedral and make sure no one was employing his predecessor's badge on new bosses. Or the boss may have been carved before 1399 and erected afterwards : we cannot believe that it was erected before. Indeed hardly any of the north side can have been complete after only five years' building. But if Walkelin built his church in sixteen years, Wykeham may have built his nave in ten : he had this advantage, that he was able to conscript labour, although he was the last Bishop to do so.

Wykeham was not by any means the last architect to try his hand on the Cathedral. Right up to the Reformation and even after it alterations **Hunton** were taking place. Prior Hunton (1470-97) built the projecting bay of the Lady Chapel with the money given him by the Queen when Henry VII's son Arthur was baptised here ; and thus made Winchester the longest Cathedral in England, and the longest mediaeval Cathedral in the world. Its total internal length is 526½ feet. Then Bishop

92

Fox (1501—1528) transformed the choir aisles
and made flying buttresses outside. He also
built the stone screens which divide the Presbytery
from the choir aisles : above them he placed the
mortuary chests which contain the bones of the
Saxon kings. The author of these lines was
fortunate enough to see inside these chests in
1932 and counted some seven skulls ; there are,
too, any number of other bones. Fox also built
the vault of the Choir, which is of wood, painted
to resemble stone, because the piers could not
support any heavier weight. The central tower
was vaulted in imitation of Fox during the Stuart
period, and the fine Norman lantern was concealed.
The woodwork and stalls of the Choir date from
the Decorated period (1308) : the pulpit is the
gift of Prior Silkstede (c. 1500), the last Prior but
two. His rebus or emblem is a skein of silk and
a black horse, a typical mediaeval pun.

One feature of the Cathedral which has not
been mentioned yet is the fine series of chantry
chapels, the finest in the kingdom. There are seven
altogether, and they offer a unique opportunity
for the study of this form of architecture. The
earliest are those of Bishops Edyngton (1366) and
Wykeham (1404) in the Nave ; then come Bishop
Waynflete (1486) and Cardinal Beaufort (1447) in
the retro-choir, Bishop Langton (1501) in the
south-east Chapel of the church, and Bishops
Fox (1528) and Gardiner (1555). Both the last
two have interesting cadavers, and Gardiner's
Chapel is a delightful combination of Renaissance
and Perpendicular work.

It may be well to recapitulate the history of the
Cathedral since Walkelin built his Norman
Minster. Lucy transformed the retro-choir :
Edyngton built the west end : Wykeham the

Nave, while Fox and Hunton altered the east end. Of the original Norman church only a section across the centre survives, comprising the transept and the crossing.

Other Churches

Besides the Cathedral there were many other churches and chapels in the town. The few that survive may be briefly dismissed.

St. Lawrence, near the City Cross, built perhaps on the site of the chapel of the Conqueror's Palace, was rebuilt in the middle of the fifteenth century. It is a quaint little relic, and here the Bishop, before his enthronement in Cathedral, changes, or used to change, his shoes, and by the same immemorial custom pays the rector £5. St. John's Church, on the skirts of St. Giles' Hill, is worthier of mention, for it contains one of the finest windows in Winchester, a lovely and massive example of geometric tracery in the south aisle. There are also St. Michael's, and St. Peter's Cheesehill, which are fair specimens of Perpendicular. But it must be understood these were only a tithe of the sacred buildings that once adorned the streets. All decayed and disappeared one by one as the prosperity and population of the place sank, leaving here and there some relic such as the name of a street, or a disused and churchless graveyard, as that of old St. Thomas', in St. Thomas Street.

See Plan, p. 12

See Diagram in Appendix

The religious houses went the same way. Hyde Abbey, moved from the New Minster by Cathedral in 1109, became degenerate like the rest—in 1325 playing at dice and chess had to be stopped. The Black Death hit the monastery hard. A relaxation of discipline followed, and by 1522 the young monks were actually practising archery in a neighbouring meadow. Now even the site is bare, but for a rubbishy remnant of a gate. The Nuns' Minster suffered in like manner at the Dissolution, and though some ruins of it stood in the seventeenth century, all is now swept away and overbuilt.

The College of St. Elizabeth of Hungary was St. Elizabeth's College in the Warden's kitchen garden ; it was sold to College at the Dissolution for £360. Meads Wall is built out of its remains. A Chapel of St. Stephen stood near by at the entrance to Gunner's Hole. Its foundations can sometimes be seen in a dry summer. There is no authority for the statement that from one of these comes the fine glass that now fills the east window of Fromond's Chantry.

Winchester started life as a Roman town, and The Walls and Gates though she has long since ceased to be a walled city, her defences were throughout the Middle Ages remarkably complete. All round the city ran a high wall with towers at intervals ; a deep fosse added to the strength of this. In a valley so well watered as this, there was no difficulty in filling the ditch, at any rate in the low-lying parts : and we shall discuss presently how the upper half of the town was dealt with in this respect. The thirteenth century witnessed important additions to the defences. It was in the second half of that century that most of the gates took their permanent shape. These were numerous enough. Besides the four main gates—the North Gate at the end of Jewry Street, the South Gate See Frontispiece at the end of Southgate Street, the West Gate and East Gate at the top and bottom of High Street—there was also the " Kyngate," next to the Close, the Castle Gate, up by the West Gate, and the Durn Gate, or Dung Gate, at the north-east corner of the Walls leading out towards Winnall. Of these, the " King's Gate " (with its little church on top) and the West Gate are the only survivors. The latter is a most interesting structure. It was built by Henry III and finished by Richard II, for the stag couchant appears upon it. The slot for the portcullis can still be seen, as can the arrangements for pouring boiling lead on the besiegers' heads. The room above the arch, originally a guardroom, has served other purposes in its time. It was once a Debtors' Prison. The inmates have left their signatures to embellish the walls. The gentlemen debtors lived there in comparative comfort, but less fortunate commoners were housed in a little hole under the floor, 4ft. 6in. in height. They were not fed, apparently, but depended on the alms of passers-by, for which they fished with bags on the end of poles. The guardroom has now been converted into a museum containing most interesting relics, some grisly enough, fetters, gyves, hanging suits, and so forth ; others connected with the municipal history, the moot horn, and the standard weights and measures. It is well worth visiting.

On the eminence immediately to the south of this gate stood the Castle. Most of it has since disappeared. The Hall, however, is fairly complete. Its walls are of Norman masonry, so we may conjecture that the fortifications also were mostly of the same date. They seem to have been immensely strong. Cromwell admitted as much when he took the Castle. In his despatch he attributed its easy capture entirely to Providence— on this occasion not without good reason. It was surrounded by a moat, the depth of which can be estimated by comparing the height of the ground level of the Hall with the drop on the east end, for the moat ran on the town side also.

How this was filled is a mystery, but the water may have been conveyed from Alresford Pond. There was a Chapel of St. Josse, a keep, a gate, and, lastly, a sally-port, still to be seen and in excellent repair. It contains two underground passages, one leading westward outside the walls ; the other, which is blocked up, appears to descend into the bowels of the earth under the town, no doubt to ascend somewhere in the region of St. Thomas' Street.

But the great Hall was its glory, a Hall which **The** has seen kings, parliaments, and even emperors, **Castle Hall** for Charles V came here. It has undergone most unfortunate changes. It was built in Norman times, was transformed by Henry III in the new Early English style, given a higher pitch to its roof, pointed windows, and two rows of Purbeck marble pillars. These were the work of Elias, of Dereham, who was also responsible for the Purbeck piers of Salisbury Cathedral. The new windows were higher than the old Norman ones, and had dormer windows with See Plate of gables breaking up into the line of the roof. Stuart The round eyes of these can still be seen inside Winchester above the apex of the present windows, but the p. 137 dormers are gone. The tracery is of later date, as is the glass, for originally only shutters were provided, of which the hinges can still be seen. The roof bears the arms of Edward IV.

At the west end rose a daïs, where Queen Victoria's statue now stands ; in the wall above it is to be seen a slit known as the King's Lug, a contrivance by which the King could overhear the consultations of his Parliament without embarrassing them with his presence. The Round Table hanging there seems to be aged enough, though it can lay no claim to having

sheltered the legs of King Arthur. One John
Harding mentions a table of the sort, and he
was born in 1378. It is painted with the names
of the Knights of the Round Table, and a highly
imaginary portrait of Arthur himself. Unluckily
the visit of Charles V rendered a new coat of
paint necessary, and it was plastered with the
blazons and colours of the houses of Lancaster
and York. The eastern addition to the Hall was
made quite lately to provide assize courts. On
the wall at that end are painted the names of
the Knights of the shire who have sat in Parliament since that institution began.

The Castle was finally demolished, as we have
said, by Cromwell. He was content, however,
with putting a grenade through the roof of the
Hall. The Hall has been till latterly in constant
use for judicial purposes, and it bears a melan-
choly memory as the place where Judge Jeffreys
condemned the unfortunate Alice Lisle. But it
must always rank with Westminster Hall, as a
place of historic importance if not of equal
architectural beauty.

Town Life in Winchester If William of Wykeham came back to Winchester, he could still find his way about the
place tolerably well, for the ground plan of the
city has changed little in five centuries.

The alleys to the north of the High Street have
become wider and more wholesome ; the inner
courtyards of taverns and rich houses have been
over-built ; the suburbs have filled the open
fields beyond the circuit of the walls, and in
general the streets follow the old lines and often
answer to the old names, but there the likeness
ends. Although we may pride ourselves on the
old-world look of the High Street, it has been
modernised out of all recognition. Little beyond

the foundations go back for more than a century or two. The quaint, old, rambling, tottering, mediaeval houses with their gaily-painted fronts, their outside stairs, and wooden galleries have long ago been swept out of existence to make way for Georgian or Stuart edifices.

Although open streams flowed down the Brook Streets and High Street, the litter and refuse was terrible and the odours unsavoury, for pigsties were erected anywhere against the house walls.

In those days the citizens lived an easy-going and haphazard existence ; and there was much loitering about the streets and gossiping in the taverns. Standing by the Market Cross one might see a motley, leisurely throng passing by— the farmer selling his produce and explaining his high prices (although a pig only cost 6d. in those days) by the toll gates at St. Swithun's Bridge : the ploughman with his ox-goad in his coarse coat of carry-marry, with his hair sticking out through holes in his hood ; the young men in jerkins and trunk hose with long bows at their backs coming back from the butts, and arguing about their scores ; the pilgrim in his ragged gown with a palm-leaf from Jerusalem or a cockle-shell from Campostella ; the College chef, a French prisoner of war from Agincourt ; the priest in beautiful vestments taking the host to some dying man, preceded by an acolyte with bell and candle ; a soldier home from the French wars in rusty armour ; the paper-maker or the butcher strolling out from their shops in Parchment or Fleshmonger Street ; the well-to-do merchant in his beaver hat and fur-lined cloak with hanging sleeves bent on business at the Guildhall, but careful to avoid the eye of a Jew who slinks along the other side of the street, a bent and cautious figure clad in a long dark robe, but prosperous enough through charging 40 per cent. on loans. Beggars, cripples, even criminals maimed by the law, bestow themselves at convenient intervals along the street. A grey Franciscan and a white Carmelite Friar compete in whining their appeal, and either is ready to shrive you for a farthing ; but both scowl when a black-robed monk from St. Swithun's strides by, with his head in the air. Presently a cavalcade will come clattering down from the Castle on its way to London, banners flying and steel flashing in the bright sun. Knights clad in armour from head to foot, but without their helmets, which are too hot, and which are borne behind by their squires. Both knight and horse are covered with trappings bearing his arms, and beside him rides his wife in a quaint pointed head-dress and brightly-coloured robes, and behind their servitors in gorgeous liveries. Another party from the Bishop's Palace will pass up to the Westgate to hawk in the park outside. If it is some feast day of the Church, we may catch sight of a procession of monks with crosses, banners, candles, and incense, chanting through the streets.

Now of the two halves into which the High Street divides the city, the southern half belonged, practically all of it, to the Church. The great close of St. Swithun covered a vast extent, and practically commanded the King's Gate. Beyond the wall, the " Soke," as it was called, was all Church property, and is now mostly College property. The south-east corner was filled by the Bishop's Palace. This leaves only the south-west corner to be occupied by the Crown : and there the Castle stood. Thus we have already two, more or less, rival authorities in Winchester. Let us now turn to the third element—the citizens themselves. We shall find them in the High Street, on the north side of the street for the most part. The richer burgesses, merchants, knights, and so forth occupied the houses in High Street itself, while the craftsmen worked in the alleys leading off it, Parchment Street, for instance, and Upper, Middle, and Lower Brook Streets ; this was the poor quarter of the town. According to the almost universal custom of the times, men of a trade collected together in one street. One may see the same phenomenon in modern Athens, where there is an alley entirely consisting of boot shops. This system of co-operation is important, for it helps us to understand how the power of the citizens gradually came to make itself felt, and, finally, was able to hold its own against the rival authorities of Crown and Church. Their chief difficulty in asserting themselves lay in the fact that, at a time when land property was everything, the actual land sites of the town were in the hands of a few owners, of which the Church was, as has been shewn, the most considerable. The strength of the burgesses lay therefore in numbers and in unity. To this end they organised themselves into a system of " gilds," or societies for mutual protection. Even the poorest joined a " gild " ; it might be the gild of his craft—carpenters or leather-workers, or what not—or it might be merely a club for supporting poorer members, or keeping up the worship of some favourite saint (and that might require a chaplain and expenditure on candles), or even to ensure a decent burial. Such present-day clubs as Oddfellows or Hearts of Oak will give a slight idea of their organisation.

But it was the gilds not of little men, but of rich merchants that really won the liberty of the burgesses. These men, driving a good trade in the wool of their Down sheep, or by importation *via* Southampton of foreign wines, formed a strong enough gild, with large funds and wide acres, such as the City Companies, Fishmongers, Cloth Workers, etc., control to this day. Little by little they won their way, receiving exemption from toll under Richard I, and at some date unknown gaining the right to elect a mayor. So municipal government was born, and the care of the city was entrusted to the Gild of Merchants meeting in conclave at the old " Gild Hall." But their troubles were not at an end. They had still some stern battles to fight with both Church and Crown. Near the Westgate was a portion of land held by the Queen as her " morning-gift " ; there the Corporation could exercise no jurisdiction. Goodbegot liberty again was exempt, and became a sanctuary for offenders against civic laws, opposite the very doors of the Gild Hall itself.

St. Giles' Fair

The most glaring example of this friction between Town and Church was St. Giles' Fair. This Fair was held every year on St. Giles' Hill, to the east of the town. No doubt it developed out of a local market, such as was held here from the earliest times. The first Royal Charter, to which it owes its conversion into a great international mart, dates from the year 1096, when William II granted " to God, to the Monastery of St. Peter, and to Walchel the Bishop, a fair at the church of St. Giles," which was to last for three days, beginning on the Eve of St. Giles (August 31st). After this the grant was confirmed, and the period of the Fair prolonged by various kings, until it was finally fixed by the Charter of Edward III in 1349 at sixteen days, beginning, as before, on August 31st. These charters gave to the Bishop the most extensive powers. During the period of the Fair all civil jurisdictions within a circuit of seven leagues were annulled, and the cases, which were normally tried by the municipal authorities or the local manorial lords, passed into the Bishop's hands. At sunrise on the Eve of St. Giles the episcopal seneschal appeared at the King's Gate, where he was met by the Mayor, bailiffs and citizens, who surrendered to him the keys. The whole cavalcade passed on to the South Gate, where the same ceremony was repeated and the Fair proclaimed. When the other gates had been visited, the seneschal, with the citizens in his train, repaired to the Pavilion Court on St. Giles' Hill. Here the seneschal, in the Bishop's name, nominated a new Mayor and bailiffs for the duration of the Fair. The Bishop's officers took complete control of the city. No shops were allowed to open and nothing might be bought or sold within seven leagues except in the enclosure of the Fair. Many men must have been needed to enforce these regulations, but in addition to this the roads leading to Winchester were carefully guarded and tolls levied on the merchants journeying to the Fair.

Meanwhile on the hill itself all was life and fun and bustle. The Fair was surrounded by a stockade with two or at the most three gates, at which the tolls could be easily collected. Inside, the ground was covered with booths, carefully arranged in rows and allotted to merchants from different countries or of different trades. Here might be seen a motley crowd of busy traffickers ;

wool merchants from London and distant Beverley and York ; Cornishmen, who sold tin and lead ; Spaniards with the finest iron ; Gascon importers of wine ; merchants from Toulouse and Flanders, Normans and Rhinelanders. In one corner were a number of booths, at which the brethren of St. Swithun's Convent drove a thriving trade in spices ; close by a royal officer might be seen purchasing cloth to make liveries for the King's household, while the bailiff of a neighbouring baron or the cellarer of a great monastery laid in a store of salted meat for the winter ; a nobleman's falconer scanned the hawks for sale ; a lady, richly clad, was tempted to purchase a peacock or an ape. Meanwhile the *aulnager* passed hither and thither to enforce the use of the standard measure of cloth, and the officers of the Fair on horseback maintained order and haled off thieves and disturbers of the peace to be dealt with at the Court of Pie Powder or Dusty Feet, where the Bishop's Justiciars sat all day to hear cases and try disputes connected with the Fair. Others again were engaged in enforcing the regulations for preventing a repetition of the fire, which in 1162 had burnt down all the booths in the Fair, together with the suburb of " Chushulle " right up to the gates of the city. Apart from those engaged in business, there was a crowd of peasants and townsmen bent only on enjoyment. Ale flowed freely, and the jester, dancer, and acrobat were much in evidence, together with many a wizard and fortune-teller.

> "There sauye I pleyen jugelours,
> Magiciens and tregetours
> And charmeresses,
> Olde wiches, sorceresses,
> That use exorsizacions,
> And eke their fumigacions."

Perhaps there would be some mystery-play, such as still survives at Oberammagau. These were grotesque travesties of Old Testament history. A large comic element kept the people in good humour. A shrew, in the character of Noah's wife, would abuse her husband on finding he had been at work on the ark for 1000 years, and all that time had kept her in the dark. There was another quaint scene in which a man in red rolled shouting across the stage to represent Abel's blood calling for vengeance. Nor were these the only occasions for jollification. Often lists would be set up and tourneys would be held, the Knights of Winchester challenging all comers, and as like as not there would be a prize for the best jouster. Competitions would be held too in archery and wrestling. Perhaps nothing throws more light on the times than the methods of administering justice ; and without going elaborately into that question, we think it is worth while to close with an account of the last " approver's " duel, which was fought here in 1456. The " approver " was a man who, to save his life, made a series of appeals against several honest men, many of whom were hanged on his evidence. His name in this case was Whithorn, a condemned thief. He was maintained at the Castle, and drew a salary of three halfpence a day from the King. At last he falsely charged one James Fisher, who challenged him to single combat. The judge laid down the following remarkable conditions. The combatants were clad all over in white sheep's leather, and were armed with a staff of green ash three feet long, provided at one end with a sharp horn of iron. If Whithorn prevailed, he would go back to prison, but have better fare than before, at the rate of 2*d.* per diem. If, on the other hand, Fisher prevailed to the extent of killing Whithorn, he was to be hanged for manslaying, " by soo moche that he hath slain the Kyngys prover." When the combat began the defendant broke his staff at the first blow, but the officers took away the approver's weapon after he had struck one return blow. Then ensued a sickening combat. The men fought with their fists and rested ; then fought and rested again. Then " they wente togedyr by the neckys," and with their teeth tore each other's leathern coats and the flesh beneath. The end seemed to have come when Whithorn cast Fisher on the ground : but in the deadly wrestle more by hap than strength, " that innocent recoveryd upon his kneys and toke that fals peler by the nose with hys tethe and put his thumb in his yee ; that fals peler cryde owte and prayde hym of mercy, for he was fals unto God and unto hym." Thus ended the duel, and the judge pronounced sentence upon the approver, whose fate is thus piously recorded, "And then he was confessyd ande hanggyd, of whos soule God have mercy. Amen."

The Sixteenth Century and After.

THE House of Lancaster never possessed any too sound claim to the throne of England, and Henry Tudor's connection even with that branch of the Royal Plantagenets was so dubious that he tried to find some excuse for being King by tracing his descent back to King Arthur, as whose lawful successor he used to pose. He carried his fantastic theory so far as to patronise the legendary capital of that ancient King, and at Winchester it was that the Houses of York and Lancaster were united in the son who was here born to Henry's Yorkist bride. The young prince was christened with great state in Winchester Cathedral, and in accordance with his father's pet theory, Arthur was his name.

This Arthur, however, died, and his brother succeeded as Henry VIII. Henry VIII seems to have had no particular love for Winchester, though the monastery here came off better than some. After the destruction of various lesser monasteries in the town, Henry's commissioners, under Thomas Cromwell, took St. Swithun's Priory in hand. Kingsmyll, the Prior, was made Dean under the new system, with a large staff. Among the treasures " given " to Cromwell were St. Swithun's costly shrine (all of whose jewels unfortunately were found to be great counterfeits), a reredos of plated gold, garnished with jewels, and a book of the Evangelists written all in gold with a cover of plated gold.

The Reformation period lost us much glass and all the statues, as well as this shrine of St. Swithun.

The Abbey of Hyde was next seen to. The Prior, Salcote, was a cunning person, who had won the King's favour by approving of the divorce. He now readily agreed with the proposal of dissolving his monastery. Next year he received the bishopric of Salisbury. Under Edward VI, this changeable prelate was a keen Reformer, and under Mary he sat in the Court that condemned Latimer and Ridley to death.

Henry VIII In the neighbourhood Henry shewed us a typical trait in his unpleasant character, for it is almost certain that he spent the night of Anne Boleyn's execution (he condescended to wear white mourning for the unfortunate lady) at Marwell Hall, then the home of the Seymours, marrying the lovely Jane there the very next day. The existing house is uninteresting, being modern Gothic, though the old garden beside it is attractive. It is situated between Owslebury and Fisher's Pond.

Mary and Philip Under Queen Mary, her favourite Bishop Gardiner held the See. To do honour to him, and because the old Faith was still firmly rooted here, the Cathedral was the scene of her unpopular marriage with Philip of Spain. Philip arrived from Southampton in a storm of rain, and was lodged in the Deanery, while the Queen was put up at Wolvesey, where Gardiner entertained her. To enter the city Philip donned a surcoat of black velvet trimmed with gold bugles, and a white velvet suit trimmed in the same way, and thus he passed the aldermen in their robes of scarlet, who knelt with gold keys on crimson cushions, and so to the grand Cathedral, which impressed the Spaniards with wonder, especially when they heard Mass sung as solemnly there as at Toledo. At the wedding, which took place two days after,

we are told that the Queen blazed with jewels
to such an extent that the eye was blinded as it
looked upon her, while her ladies looked more
like celestial angels than mortal creatures.

Winchester was not at all Protestant, which
accounts for the fact that only one burning took
place here during Mary's reign, that of Benbridge.
Under Elizabeth, Robert Horne, who was a
Puritan, ruled the Diocese with a rod of iron.
He stripped the lead off the roof of the Cathedral,
and destroyed the Norman Chapter House.

With James I's reign Winchester came once **James I**
more into prominence for a brief space. In 1603
the Plague was raging in London, and the Law
Courts were removed to Winchester, where the
charge of plotting against James with the intention of placing Lady Arabella Stuart upon the
throne was brought against several gentlemen,
Brooke, Cobham, Grey, Markham, and notably
Sir Walter Raleigh.

The King, being pro-Spanish and jealous of
Elizabethan favourites, hated Sir Walter, and **Raleigh's**
since his good nature and generosity had so far **Trial**
made him extremely popular, the King had
public opinion on his side. A contemporary
writer chronicles with astonishment the bitter-
ness of the mob, who surrounded Raleigh's coach
on his way to Winchester for trial ; but we learn
from the same authority that " he neglected and
scorned it from such base and rascal people."
The trial was a shameful farce, and the behaviour
of Coke, the chief prosecutor, insufferable.
Raleigh was condemned to death on very insufficient evidence, and a few days later saw an
extraordinary tragi-comedy played in the Castle
yard. Through the grey haze of the drizzling
December day, he saw Cobham, Grey, and

Markham ascend a scaffold to share the fate of Brooke, who, a few days previously, had been executed for complicity in the plot. One after another they prepared for death : then each in turn was led away, none of them thinking that there was any chance of a reprieve. However, the three were brought back on to the scaffold and informed of his Majesty's gracious pleasure that they should not die. This foolish farce was typical of James, the Wisest Fool in Christendom, for, as he had foreseen, it set people talking about the gracious mercy and unheard-of clemency of the man whom they perversely called a second Solomon. Raleigh, who had spent the time since his condemnation in begging for a reprieve on any conditions whatever, was now informed that he should not be put to death. Nevertheless, he was beheaded on the same charge fifteen years later.

See Plan, p. 123

The early years of Charles I's reign passed by in Winchester with comparative quietude. Laud, in his great work of righting the Church of England, found some fault with our Chapel services, and put an end to the use of the Cathedral nave as a thoroughfare by having a way pierced through the buttress at the south-west of the Close, with the curious inscription pointing out the way of pedestrian and worshipper respectively.

[This runs :—

ILL	PREC
AC	ATOR
H	VI
AMBULA	

and is to be seen on the south corner of the west Front.]

Civil War At the start of the Civil War, Winchester was undoubtedly Royalist in sympathy, but very soon fell into the hands of the enemy, being seized by the Parliamentarian General, Sir William Waller, in 1642. He was soon made General of Hampshire, and this County, with the exception of Basing House, which was held for so long by Lord Winchester, remained for about a year under his control. However, no garrison seems to have been left in Winchester, and it was presently seized by Lord Ogle, who was then reinforced by the famous Royalist General, Lord Hopton, who would have soon brought the city entirely back to their allegiance. But meanwhile Sir William Waller from his headquarters at Farnham surprised Colonel Boles, who lay at Alton with 1300 men. He retired into the town church with eighty men, and was slain fighting bravely in the pulpit. The bullet-marks may be seen to-day on the walls of the building. We are told, on an inconspicuous brass to the gallant Colonel's memory in Winchester Cathedral, that when his gracious Sovereign heard of his death he cried, " Bring me a ' moorning ' scarf, for I have lost one of the best commanders in the kingdom."

ERRATUM.

For reference note ' See Plan p. 123 ' *read* ' See Plan p. 137.'

strongly held by Ogle, and had to be content with plundering and devastating the city. The Cathedral he had desecrated before, by riding up to the altar with his troops in full war equipment.

At length, in 1654, when the Royal cause had finally been lost in the Battle of Naseby, Oliver Cromwell turned his attention to Winchester, pitching his tents by the clump of trees which now bears his name. He was soon inside the walls, and took possession of the Castle, which he began to blow up with gunpowder. What was left of it was given to Waller as his share in the work of destruction. Cromwell also finally abolished the use of the Anglican liturgy in Cathedral, and substituted a thing called the directory. Under him Wolvesey Castle was also reduced to its present state. Winchester has no cause to be grateful to Oliver Cromwell.

During this stormy period a certain Colonel Fiennes, an Old Wykehamist, saved from defacement both Wykeham's Chapel and College, even including the statue of the Virgin on Outer Gate. Such a statue left intact is quite a phenomenon in this country. "Out of the brass torn from the monuments violated in Cathedral," says Bruno Ryves, "a house as strong as the brazen towers of old romance might have been built."

It was proposed to pull down the Church of Holy Trinity, as they called the Cathedral during the Commonwealth, but a carefully worded petition from the citizens put an end to this project. It was, however, left in the bad state of which Waller's men were the cause. The Cathedral Muniment House was twice ransacked by Parliamentary soldiers, and several old documents lost. Consequently, in spite of the devoted labour of John Chase, the Chapter Clerk, many treasures were lost to the Cathedral. Fortunately, however, some of the books were granted by Parliament to College, and were returned to the Dean and Chapter after the Restoration.

Winchester had one more visit from her King, upon which he is reported to have cured one of the crowd of the disease known as the King's Evil. It had always been very loyal to the unhappy Charles (having actually given £30,000, as well as the city plate to his cause, and it never got any reward save the portrait of Charles II in the Guildhall), and when he came on his last sad journey through the town two months before his execution, the Mayor and Corporation appeared in state to do him honour as their king, in spite of the annoyance of his captors.

In 1665, when the plague visited London, Charles II came down to Winchester, but it followed him here before long, and he was obliged to go away again. The plague was particularly bad, and very many died. The country folk used to leave their goods on a stone outside the West Gate and go away. Thereupon the townspeople came and removed them, leaving their money, which the others dipped in vinegar and pocketed.

Charles II was very fond of Winchester, and further on we shall have more to say of this phase in its history. It was this King who once paid Richard Cromwell, formerly Protector (who now lived in retirement three miles away at Hursley), a pleasant surprise visit. Though a very feeble despot, he made an excellent squire, and did not die till the reign of Queen Anne, when he had reached the age of eighty-six. His death is recorded with those of the rest of his family on a large pillared monument of marble in the tower of Hursley Church, with never a mention of the exalted position he had once occupied for so short a time.

The last important chapter in the history of Winchester is also the most disgraceful. It was here that Judge Jeffreys committed perhaps the most atrocious crime out of an unparalleled series, when he sentenced the aged Lady Lisle to be burned, for harbouring one of Monmouth's rebels. In spite of all the appeals of the Dean and Chapter, James and Jeffreys would only commute the sentence of burning to one of beheading, which was accordingly carried out in the Square where a museum now stands.

From that time the lot of Winchester has been the same as that of other small and sleepy Cathedral cities.

Text-books upon architecture separate the time since the decay of the Gothic into two ages— the Age of the Renaissance and the Age of Revivals. The Renaissance began of course in Italy. The writings of Petrarch (1304—1374) inspired men of learning, and especially young men, to look back across the ten centuries and more of dark and middle ages, to the high civilisation and polished style of ancient Rome and Greece. In Florence, Venice and other cities of the north, the study of classical Latin and later of Greek itself, became the passion and *sine qua non* of every courtier. But it was less easy to begin afresh in art than in learning. Artistic success is only made possible by craftsmanship, and craftsmanship by a long and tedious training. Craftsmen are by nature conservative, clinging to tradition, unwilling to experiment with unknown materials and unaccustomed styles. Architecture and painting, therefore, lagged behind language, and the first sign of the break with the Gothic tradition of building does not appear till about 1430, and then in Florence. The leader of the new school of architects was Filippo Brunelleschi. He was enthralled by the dignity of the ancient buildings of Rome and determined to reintroduce something of their simplicity, symmetry and shape. The palaces executed for the great merchant families, Medici, Pitti and the rest, are the splendid fruit of this first *renaissance* of Roman architecture. From Florence the new style spread, a style with all the freedom but none of the finicalness of Gothic.

In about 1470, however, a new influence was **Vitruvius** introduced. A manuscript of a work by Vitruvius, an amateur architect of the time of Augustus, was discovered in Switzerland. Herein Vitruvius gave exact values for the proportions of each columnar order—Doric, Ionic and Corinthian—how great in proportion to the column's height, that is, most be its thickness, capital and architrave. A new school of pedantic architects arose ; design became founded on the column only and a style intended for halls and temples was employed unthinkingly for churches, town houses and country villas. This columnar style reached its zenith of magnificence in Michael Angelo's east end and dome of St. Peter's.

The cult of the Classics now swept over the **Renaissance** Alps, and Francois I invited Italian artists of the **Architecture** highest talent to his court. But in France **in France** Gothic building was a native art ; its influence, despite its decadence, was still enormous ; all the craftsmen had been trained in the Gothic school. Early French Renaissance architecture is a brilliant blend of the old and the new, using, with the freakishness of the Gothic, Classical columns and pilasters, all with bases and entablatures complete, pediments and round-arched arcades and that beautiful wall ornament in low relief to be seen framing the doorways to the presbytery in Winchester Cathedral. The chateau of Chambord near the Loire is typical of this early Renaissance style, the Palais du Luxembourg of the " purer " Italian style which replaced it in the 17th century.

Gradual passing of Middle Ages in England The sketch of the development of architecture abroad has of necessity been long ; for Italy was the spring of the waters of new art and the stream flowed to us through France.

But whereas French Gothic was quite worn out in 1500, the English was lively still and received the Classical inspiration more to refresh than revive. Long before the Wars of the Roses the uncomfortable castle style of building had given way to a new type of country house. Penshurst Place in Kent, built in 1388 by a rich London merchant, was perhaps the first of these. It was unfortified and comfortable with big windows and a pleasure park. The Wars of the Roses confirmed the priority of this new type of country gentleman. The quarrelsome and conservative feudal nobility frittered away its life and means in a struggle which only resulted in the triumph of its worst enemy, the Tudor dynasty. The Tudors were intellectual and somewhat parvenu ; they hastened to transfer the property first of the old nobility and then of the Church into the hands of persons like themselves, clever, scheming and modern. England woke up, rich men attained a new and European elegance of living, Latin and Greek flowered again at the Universities. But the Italian villa style of building did not at once replace the English manor house of the fifteenth century ; just as in France the old form remained, embellished with lovely Classical details

116

and improved by a Classical magnificence and symmetry.

The growing influence of the Italian Renaissance can be traced with ease. In 1511 Torrigiano came to England and in the great mortuary chapel of Henry VII at Westminster, which is the culmination of Gothic architecture in England, made of the royal tomb the first truly Renaissance work we knew. The smart new manner quickly spread from London ; columns appeared everywhere in porches and fireplaces, doorways, panelling and furniture. Bramshill and The Vyne near Basingstoke, and Wilton and Longford near Salisbury testify to the beauty and elegance of the great Elizabethan and Jacobean houses. More famous still are Longleat in Wiltshire ; Hatfield and Burleigh House, the mansions of the Cecils ; and the royal palace of Nonsuch in Surrey, long since destroyed. These houses were all built round inner courts and the rooms were reached by a number of small stairways as they are still in the Colleges of Oxford and Cambridge. In 1620 the modern system of a great interior staircase and of corridors on each storey off which the rooms led was invented at Blickling in Norfolk and speedily gained favour.

Renaissance Architecture in England 1512—1620

The development of English architecture from 1620 to 1650 is due mostly to the genius of one man, Inigo Jones. Jones was trained in the Elizabethan school with its Gothic affinities, and as a young man designed buildings in this style. But visits to Italy in 1603 and 1613 persuaded him to introduce into England that severe and noble Italian manner which Palladio had developed from the writings of Vitruvius. Many buildings in England, in London especially, were erected or altered in this manner by Jones. An addition

Inigo Jones 1620—1650

117

to Wilton House is his. A design for a Royal palace at Whitehall was developed by Jones and his pupil Webb which was gigantic in scale and imperial in dignity. It is not surprising that neither Charles nor James could raise the money to begin the work, but it is sad at the same time that the present sovereign and his Government do not occupy a palace vaster and nobler than the world has ever seen. Only the beautiful Banqueting House was made, less than a fiftieth part of the whole design.

Sir Chris=
topher Wren
1650—1710

Wren was a mathematician and astronomer by training and profession, an architect by virtue of his talents and his taste. On the grand scale St. Paul's is evidence of his power, on the small the city churches of his ingenuity. But above all he excelled in the designing of country and town houses. Belton House in Lancashire is a magnificent example of his work. He revived the use of brick and stone together and never sacrificed convenience to effect. This tradition of fine honest building survived Wren far into the eighteenth century.

Baroque

Vanbrugh
1710—1730

Meanwhile in Europe Palladian architecture, made to onerous rules which only the greatest dared to flout, had become stale. To achieve new effect the Baroco was invented in Italy and spread to France and Germany. Baroque is more a manner than a style and depends on those qualities of ostentation, unexpectedness and asymmetry that appeal to the dramatic sense. In England it is hardly found save in the work of Vanbrugh, the playwright, between 1700 and 1730. The enormous palaces of Castle Howard, Blenheim, Stowe and Seaton Delaval are typical of the period. Each cost a quarter of a million of taxpayers' money. In spite of unrivalled parkland settings and melodramatic skylines, there is something unsatisfactory in them all, at least beside the austere and noble Pitti Palace at Florence.

But a reaction against the dramatic baroque of Vanbrugh set in. Lord Burlington and Kent in London and the Woods at Bath brought architecture back to the strict Palladian rule. Bath is a treasury of wonderful buildings of the eighteenth century. At the same time the taste for " roccoco " developed in England. Although houses were still solid and severe, the polite world allowed its taste for the pretty and curious to find architectural expression in a host of strange temples and grottoes about their grounds. All kinds are to be seen about Stowe School near Buckingham : a gingerbread Gothic temple, a dank and gimcrack grotto sunk amid the roots of trees, a Greek temple, a Roman temple, a copy of Inigo Jones' lovely covered bridge at Wilton ; only the Chinese pagoda in the lake has disappeared. <sub/>

Georgian and Roccoco

In the second half of the eighteenth century Greek influence is paramount. The brothers Adam introduced a new grace into interior decoration and furniture by adapting ornament from Classical Greek buildings to the Georgian house. A vast amount of work has been left by them in London, Edinburgh and many country houses.

Greek Influence
The Adams

From 1800 to 1830 one man dominated London architecture, John Nash. He did not invent but certainly did stablish the use of plaster and paint as a finish to a " Grecian " building. Old Regent's Quadrant, where Regent Street meets Piccadilly, has now disappeared, and was probably his best work ; but in Waterloo Place, in Carlton

Nash
1800—1830

House Terrace, and in the buildings round Regent's Park his work is richly represented. These, columns and arches and pediments included, are all built of brick with a layer of plaster painted creamy-white to give a marble look. Some of his terraces are magnificent in composition but their upkeep is of course expensive.

A number of monumental buildings of great grandeur were erected before 1840 ; amongst others the British Museum, the London University and St. George's Hall at Liverpool. Town and country houses were mostly dignified and comfortable, built sometimes of stone but usually of brick plastered over and then painted or stuccoed.

The "Gothic" Revival

Meanwhile a ghastly poison was working underground. The revival of the Gothic style began in the country as the whim of the rich and dilettanti. But the completion in 1778 of his Gothic mansion at Strawberry Hill by the witty and affected Horace Walpole pointed the way to further eccentricities. A reliable architect named James Wyatt turned his attention from Classical to Gothic architecture, and found no lack of clients. His most ambitious work was the erection in 1798 of Fonthill Abbey in Wiltshire for a millionaire named William Beckford. This was a sham Gothic monastery, partly entire and partly in ruins, with a great octagonal centre tower and an entrance hall with a vault as high as Westminster Abbey.

The "Gothic" of the 19th Century

With the spread of the Romantic movement in literature, led by Goethe, Walter Scott and Byron, the interest in things mediaeval became increasingly wide. From 1820 onwards churches have been almost exclusively erected in some kind of

Gothic style. Before 1840 or 1850, however, the revival of interest in Gothic architecture did not much influence the plan or appearance of public or domestic buildings. These remained on the whole sensible, commodious and unadorned. London, the spas, the coast resorts and the country towns are all rich in buildings of this period.

But about 1850 " Gothic " became the favourite style of architects, and seemingly of public too. Few houses or public buildings have much merit until quite recent times, in which Sir Edwin Lutyens and others have brought back both dignity and beauty to their art.

It is to be hoped that public bodies and private persons alike will not be afraid in the future to build in a *truly* modern style and will not for ever be content unsuitably and even foolishly to ape the past.

There are examples of all classes of building between 1500 and to-day in the city. The period 1500—1600 is somewhat poorly represented, but there are plenty of examples of Tudor building in houses and churches in the country. The architecture of the next three centuries is quite well illustrated.

Renaissance Architecture in Winchester

The best piece of Tudor work in Winchester is the fine old house, let into the Close wall, and known as Cheyney Court. It has picturesque carved gables, and the old barge-boards used in its construction should be noticed. Another of the most picturesque corners in the town is formed by that part of God-Begot House, which was

Tudor Buildings

built in 1558, and by its upper storey timbered with splendid old beams hanging over a narrow alley.

Cottages   Perhaps a reference to the country cottages at such villages near here as Tichborne and Cheriton, with their over-hanging thatched eaves, which must have been built in the Tudor period, may not be out of place, while we must mention the beautiful red-brick farm of Elizabethan date, which stands by the River Itchen between Eastleigh and Twyford. In Winchester itself there are many pretty cottages plastered over in shades varying between pink and cream colour, notably between Cathedral and Southgate Street, and near St. John's Church.

We must not omit two very interesting fragments of Renaissance architecture to be found in the neighbourhood of Hyde Abbey. The first of these is a remarkably fine Renaissance doorway with pilasters and pediment. It stands on the right of the Worthy Road, and is now blocked up. It is of early date, and is entirely of brick. The brickwork is in English bond. From 1600 until quite recently Flemish bond has been almost exclusively used in brick buildings. The difference between the styles is illustrated at the end of the book.

The other fragment near Hyde is very interesting. It is a curious stone ornamentation that once crowned a garden gate, now sunk deep into the ground beside the lane where it is to be found. On the stone are curious carvings, consisting apparently of cartwheels, miniature battlements turned upside down, and a geometrical figure with typical, though defaced, obelisks crowning the whole erection. Why the space between the stone ornamentation and the oak beam, which must have been the top of the gate, should be so large, is a mystery.

We have mentioned Inigo Jones, who lived in the Inigo Jones Early Stuart period, as a very great architect. We have none of his work at present in Winchester, but for some time there stood in the Cathedral, dividing nave and choir, a screen of white stone, designed by him, with delicate pillars and statues of Charles I and James I in niches at each side. These statues by Le Sueur, the sculptor who made Charles' famous statue in Whitehall, are now on each side of the west door. The bodies clad in armour were cast in the same mould. This screen has been replaced by a modern Gothic work matching the choir stalls.

When Charles I visited the city, a medallion of his face and his Queen's was put on the wooden vaulting of the tower, where it may still be seen. This vaulting is good, but an open lantern over the crossing would be infinitely more magnificent.

The unrepaired ravages committed by Parliamentarian soldiers in the Close at the taking of Winchester had made it necessary, on Charles II's restoration, to make great changes. Accordingly the aspect of the ruined monastery was changed into that of the picturesque Close of to-day. The Prior's lodging was carved out into rooms, The Deanery and a staircase was put into it, while the three arches built in the time of Henry III formed the stately porch. This is how the Deanery was formed.

Now, too, most of the Canons' houses were Houses in built. The present Pilgrims' School, which had the Close been built into the Guest Hall in Tudor times, was now restored, no doubt by the same workmen as built School, as it contains a frieze exactly similar to that in School. Dome Alley was built now of red brick, with its projecting brick cornice, to which the long row of sharp-pointed gables was subsequently added. These houses are also graced by Tudor waterpipes, engraved with the Tudor rose and the arms of the Diocese, as well as other devices, including grapes. These must have come off some earlier building. The picturesque and irregular appearance of many houses in the Close make them look of older date than the time of Charles II, and, of course, in material and foundation they often are. Architecture did not become prim and regular until Lord Burlington and the eighteenth century.

When King Charles II began to frequent Winchester, he chose it originally as being a suitable place from which to organise great hunting parties in the New Forest, and he used often to ride or even walk thither. He took a peculiar liking for the place, and in his visits to the town he used to improvise dwellings for his **Quarters of** court either by quartering them on unwilling **Charles II's** inhabitants, or else by buying up and hiring **Court** various houses for them all over the town. The Duke of Buckingham, son of the ill-fated favourite of Charles I, and one of Charles II's greatest friends, with a character fully doubtful enough to recommend him to that monarch, lived in the large white house, now 8 and 9 Kingsgate Street. James, Duke of York, lived in the house in St. Swithun's Street, where Symonds Street joins it. This was built by Sir Christopher Wren, and has been spoilt by the addition of a Victorian bay window on the ground floor. The unfortunate Queen, Catherine of Portugal, lived in a house still to be seen at the corner of Canon Street and St. Cross Road. It is a strange, irregular house, covered with cream-coloured plaster, chiefly remarkable for its extraordinary lack of windows ; this is made up for by one large projecting bow-window of wood, painted dark green, which has been put on since Catherine's day.

Charles himself lodged at the Deanery. His host was one Meggott, called the " bowing Dean," presumably so named from his cringing, subservient behaviour to the King. The beautiful red-brick gallery of the house was probably built out into the garden for the Royal use by Dean Clarke, near which, we are told, there was once a room built for Nell Gwynne. The tale which hangs thereby is perhaps too well known to need repetition. Prebendary Ken was **Ken** requested to put her up in his house, which stood in what is now the Deanery Garden. He firmly refused to do anything of the kind, to the horror and consternation of the " bowing Dean," who regarded it as sacrilege to disobey an anointed King, even if his character was no better than was Charles II's. But it was not to Meggott, whom he must have heartily despised, that the King gave the next vacant bishopric : it was to " the ugly little man who wouldn't give poor Nelly a lodging." Nell Gwynne seems to have owned a house at the town end of St. Peter Street, which has been largely restored and presents a square, yellow appearance, with new windows, though two old ones may be seen in it.

We do not know how the luxurious court of Charles II liked their improvised quarters in a provincial town, but we can guess that they did not share the pleasure felt by the King in his latest whim. They had, however, hopes of more suitable quarters in the future. Charles had **Wren's** ordered Dr. Christopher Wren to build him a **Palace**

palace on the hill west of Cathedral, with all speed, and he completed a large portion of it. During its erection Charles's visits became more and more frequent, and his delight in the plan increased. He wished Winchester to rival Versailles. Wren's design for the palace consisted of a massive brick block, with a portico in the centre, composed of four marble pillars and two pilasters ; above this an octagonal dome, or cupola, of great height, from which the King might be able to see his men-of-war riding at anchor at Spithead. A wing on either side was to be connected with the main body by a colonnade ; the chief feature of each wing was a Royal Chapel, one for the King, one for the Queen, each two storeys high, with a small cupola, also octagonal, on top.

From the Cathedral west front to the Palace terrace, a distance of about a quarter of a mile, Charles and Wren planned a stately approach perfectly straight, with rows of trees on either side, statues and fountains, and flights of wide, shallow steps in the approved style of the French Renaissance. Down this triumphal way the King was to come in procession on great festivals, preceded by his court and the Cathedral clergy. Nor was this an end to the Royal scheme. All the slopes to the south of the Palace, as far as St. Cross and Oliver's Battery, were ordered to be kept during the King's pleasure, for here he intended to make a great park or pleasaunce with groups of fine trees. And this, on the whole, is the most pleasing part of the scheme, for in other ways it is perhaps well that Charles' death intercepted all these fine plans. A fine effect, it is true, might have been obtained, at the expense, however, of both city and cathedral. The city would have become a mere Windsor, Potsdam, or Versailles, the Cathedral a mere appendage to a palace.

The King's House, as it was called, remained incomplete for 200 years, till it was burnt down in 1894. Very various opinions were expressed about it during the period. Anne and her husband, George of Denmark, had thought of completing it, but when they came to see it, and had a special outside staircase constructed for them, they thought Windsor far preferable. It then remained disused for a long while. When Horace Walpole saw it, he wrote that he liked it less than any other building of Wren's he had ever seen. It was, he said, a mixture between a town hall and hospital in appearance. Fanny Burney admired its appearance and position, and thinking it a great pity that such a building should be left useless, determined to use her influence with Queen Charlotte and have it converted into a hospital. We next, however, hear of it as a place for French prisoners of war, and after that it was converted into barracks, and remained so till its destruction.

To return to the days of Charles II, while Sir Christopher Wren was superintending the erection of Charles' palace, he found plenty of time to build elsewhere in Winchester, and there are a great many houses here which were probably **Houses by** built by him, though in most cases it cannot be **Wren** proved. The Duke of York's House certainly was built from his design, and the likeness of its windows leads us to suppose that he may have built also a very fine house of the same period in Southgate Street. Next to this house there is another very striking house of the period with a fine porch. It is largely covered with ivy.

The question as to who was the architect of School is still a disputed one. The windows and much of the exterior ornamentation of School are precisely similar to those of St. Benet's Church, Upper Thames Street, London, which is known to have been built in 1683 by Strong, under Wren's direction. About this time Strong came down to Winchester to build Charles II's Palace ; and it has been suggested that he may have been employed also to build School, which was begun in 1684. Even so, and assuming that he reproduced in School the designs made by Wren for St. Benet's Church, there is no definite proof that Wren actually supervised the erection of School, though many eminent authorities hold the view that he did.

Though its style does not go well with the grey buildings of Wykeham, School is the most remarkable piece of architecture at Winchester College. There are many other Perpendicular buildings with considerable resemblance to ours here, but School is really unique, and in judging it, we must not forget that the side from Meads was not meant to be seen. Bearing this in mind, we cannot deny the stateliness of the six tall, corniced windows and the finely carved door, surmounted by Cibber's statue of the Founder.

This is one of the two most considerable Renaissance buildings in Winchester. The other is the partly demolished Wolvesey Palace, which we know is Wren's. It is wholly of stone, which is remarkable here where most of the buildings are only faced with it. Bishop Morley, we are told, accompanied Charles II on his travels : however, he was a very saintly man, and to him we owe the present house. When translated to Winchester from Worcester, he brought with him his famous friend, Izaak Walton, and soon afterwards made Thomas Ken his chaplain. In original design his palace was far more imposing than it is now, and most of it was completed, though not in Morley's lifetime. The main body of the Palace extended eastward, making an imposing façade towards College Street and hiding the Castle ruins. Sir Jonathan Trelawny, the famous hero of the song about the 20,000 Cornishmen, finished the west wing which joined the main body of the Palace to the Castle Chapel. This is a building of great dignity, whose foundations and lower walls are Norman but whose upper part, including the windows, is late fifteenth century. Bishop Morley had it paved with black and white marble, which still remains. After a period of inexcusable neglect from intervening Bishops, the beautiful façade and eastern wing of Morley's Palace was pulled down in 1781 by Bishop Brownlow North, who did not want the expense of keeping it up. The west wing, or present building, was left. Its unimportance in comparison with the rest of the building is strikingly shewn by Dr. Milner's description of it as " certain offices at the west end."

In 1927 Bishop Woods returned to Wolvesey. The Bishops of Winchester had made Farnham Castle their Palace for at least 800 years, but Farnham is now part of the newly-created Diocese of Guildford. It was considered also more fitting that the Bishop should live in the Cathedral city of his See, and Wolvesey, in spite of its diminished glory, is still a magnificent building and well worthy of the fifth prelate in the kingdom.

Other fine houses of the period are Avebury **Other** House, in Saint Peter Street : the Pilgrims' **Buildings** School, No. 3, in the Close : the Warden's house, rather spoilt by its modern Gothic flint façade, and No. 9 Parchment Street, which has a most peculiar round-topped porch, hollowed out beneath the arch.

In 1711, the old Guildhall, now business premises, was built, with its fine projecting clock of carved oak and its strange wooden cupola. In 1713, the remarkably unflattering statue of Queen Anne was added to the building, where it still stands.

Domestic Architecture in Winches=ter since Queen Anne It is customary to suppose the progress of architecture during the last two centuries a subject of such tedium and horror intermixed as to be unworthy of any kind of study. This is an over-statement. Save in the black years between 1860 and 1890 good buildings in greater or less numbers have appeared.

Georgian and Regency 1730—1830 Typical Georgian houses of the middle period (1730—1770) are to be found in Kingsgate Street (*e.g.* 13, 14, 15, 16 and Witham Close), in College Street, St. Peter Street, High Street, Jewry Street and others. They are mostly built of good red brick, square, with plain sash windows, brick cornices, and fine front doorways with fanlights and pediments or projecting porches. The Market Hall (now Messrs. Dumpers) and the new front of the old Guildhall (below the clock) were both built about 1772 and represent the last phase of the Georgian. They are made of brick with stone pilasters and cornices in the Greek manner.

Of the " brick and stucco " style which followed four rows of houses at the Broadway end of Eastgate Street provide a good example. Their dates are approximately 1800, 1810, 1820 and 1830. The latest has some pseudo-mediaeval ornament. The villas in Grafton Road (1820), St. James' and Clifton Terraces (1830's and 1846), overlooking the railway, various houses in St. James' Hill and St. Cross Road and the plastered part of " K " House are of this period. The Corn Exchange in Jewry Street was built in 1838 and is an exaggeratedly Italianate building with wide spreading eaves and a low-pitched roof. Numbers 60 to 86 in Southgate Street are typical of London building of the '30's. Sunnyside (I House) was built in 1842.

Meanwhile the Gothic was gaining in popular favour. There are a number of extremely interesting early Gothic Revival buildings in Winchester, all built about 1790 : two cottages in Jewry Street, the main facade of the Mayor's House in Broadway and Dr. Milner's Roman Catholic Chapel between Jewry and St. Peter's Streets. The almshouses of St. John's Hospital on the south side of Broadway were built in the 1830's, those on the north in the 1850's. St. Maurice's Church (restored 1932) belongs to about 1850 and so does the Gas Company's building opposite the Black Swan. Examples of Victorian villas, mostly more or less in the " Gothic " style, are to be found along Christ Church Road and upon St. Giles' Hill. Gothic Revival 1790—to-day

The Houses C (1862), D (1868), E (1869), G and H were built between 1860 and 1869, and Class Rooms were converted by Butterfield in 1868. The exterior of the last building is neither ugly nor mean, but inside the rooms are mostly ill-ventilated and dark. The design for the Sanatorium buildings won a prize in 1872, though to what feature success was due is not easy to decide. Gymnasium and Rackets Courts (1895) almost exceed Sanatorium in senseless ugliness. Victorian Gothic of College

In 1873 the new Guildhall was erected. This is a sermon in stone, wherein the doctrine of Ruskin Guildhall 1873 is preached. It is extremely similar to the Oxford Museum (*c.* 1860) and is meant to express in English material the beauties of the Venetian Gothic of the 13th century. The facade is lavishly provided with all the abracadabra of pointed arches, polished granite pillars, sculptured tympana and piebald archivolts. It is quite fine. The sides, rear, high-pitched roof of blue and purple slate, and the skinny oblong central tower are all unspeakably abominable. So is the interior. The " Early English " Free Library next door was built in 1876 and its detail is similar to de Lucy's work in Cathedral. About this time (1876) the County Hospital beside the Romsey Road was built of red brick with chequer ornament in blue ; the windows have stone tracery and conform to the late 13th century Geometrical style.

Recent
Building

Of post-War domestic building in Winchester the most important is the Stanmore Housing Scheme. The Elementary School beside the railway is an admirable building. So also is a house called " Marlfield " at the top of St. James' Hill.

War
Memorial
Cloister

The College War Memorial Cloister was designed by Sir Herbert Baker and completed in 1922. The whole structure is floating upon a concrete raft in the waterlogged gravel below. Sir Herbert describes the Cloister as " Elemental " in style. It is one of the most famous of School Memorials and has won golden opinions from all sorts of people.

Cathedral

In Queen Anne's time some alterations were made in the choir of the Cathedral, where, of course, the most striking features of the Renaissance must always be the handsome stone screens supporting the chests which contain the bones of the Anglo-Saxon Kings. These screens, which were put up by Bishop Fox, were made, as Blomfield points out, by Perpendicular craftsmen, while the numerous and delicate mouldings are all Renaissance. In 1713 the choir level was raised ; it was paved with that curious pattern of grey and white marble which is still to be seen, though it has now grown lustreless through lack of polish. We must suppose it offered a more striking appearance then, as it seems to have impressed a writer of the 18th century more than anything else in the church. The carved oak Altar-rail, one of the works of Grinling Gibbons, to whom we owe the richly-carved stalls in St. Paul's Cathedral, had been put up some years before. The Altar-books were given by Charles II. In his reign, too, the Cathedral Library over the ancient Slype was rebuilt. The books, and the magnificent cases in which they rest, were the bequest of good Bishop Morley, having formed part of his own private collection.

Besides the features in the Cathedral of that period, which still remain, there were others of the eighteenth century which are no longer to be seen. The above-mentioned screen by Inigo Jones divided Nave from Choir, a vast oak throne of the Corinthian order stood in the place of the modern one, and above the altar stood a huge wooden erection with columns and gilt capitals. To crown all, in the niches of the great reredos, then empty, stood black and gold funeral urns.

Round the Nave also was rising a series of monuments, mostly bad and of doubtful fitness in their Gothic surroundings. The most considerable monument of the period, at any rate in size, in Winchester Cathedral is immediately on our left as we enter the south door. It was designed by Cheere in memory of Bishop Willis, who, we learn, was a mild and gentle man, but a terrible Whig preacher, and died in 1734. Beneath an exceedingly elaborate marble cornice and pediment, supported by two richly carved columns, Bishop Willis lies in his robes in a theatrical pose on a sarcophagus, which stands on two extraordinary marble feet, with toes each the size of a potato. A great piece of a column has been hollowed out in the erection of Bishop Hoadly's monument, and there it stands by the daïs outside the choir-screen, a tablet of marble with Hoadly's bewigged and uninspiring profile above it, and a whole pillar spoiled in its making. Hoadly himself was a very able but extremely unpopular prelate, and a keen Whig controversialist.

Hoadly

It is interesting to know that George II had a poor opinion of him ; for he once referred to him, when speaking to the Queen, in the following uncomplimentary terms : " Well madam, if the Bishop of Winchester is your friend, you have a great puppy and a very dull fellow and a very great rascal for your friend." But perhaps an accusation of rascality from so hardened a reprobate as George II does not carry very great weight.

During the early years of the 19th century considerable anxiety was felt for the stability of the Cathedral and extensive repairs were carried out, both on the roof and in the nave ; they were completed in 1825. In 1820 the ceiling was put in the South Transept, also a screen and gallery dividing the latter from the choir.

Until 1825 the organ-case had been in Renaissance style ; in this year Edward Blore substituted the present case, which was thought to harmonise better with the woodwork of the choir-stalls. In 1853 it was decided to purchase a new organ. This was supplied by the firm of Willis, and had been shown at the Great Exhibition of 1851. It had to be reduced from 70 stops to 49, to fit the existing case. It has subsequently been rebuilt on two occasions, and is supposed to compare very favourably with more modern organs.

In 1827 the existing Bishop's chair was erected ; seven years earlier Inigo Jones' choir-screen had been removed, and the statues of James I and Charles I, which it contained, were placed at the west end. A new wooden screen was erected, but in 1874 the Chapter gave orders for the removal of this, and the erection of a new screen harmonising with the stalls, as a joint memorial to Bishop Wilberforce and Dean Garnier. It was carried out by Sir Gilbert Scott, who also designed the memorial to Bishop Wilberforce in the South Transept.

In 1820 Dr. Nott had removed the " Grecian urns " which then decorated the reredos, the niches of which remained empty for more than 50 years. In 1885 a thorough cleaning and repairing of the structure was begun and in 1888 the niches began to be filled with statues and statuettes. By 1891 the reredos had acquired its present appearance at a total cost of £5,400.

From 1905 to 1912 very extensive underpinning became necessary on the south side, and a diver was employed to carry out the work. New buttresses also had to be erected to support the wall of the south aisle ; at the same time the vaulting of the nave was reset. Details of the repairs are inscribed on the inside wall of the west end of the Cathedral.

After the Great War various War Memorials and Rolls of Honour were placed in the Cathedral, and in 1923 a painted wooden statue of Joan of Arc was erected at the entrance of the Lady Chapel, under Dean Hutton's direction, as a gesture of friendship to our late allies the French.

In recent years Professor Tristram has restored the mortuary chests in the chancel and the frescoes behind the organ, which were painted *c*. 1220. In 1930 the "Friends of the Cathedral" were founded by Dean Selwyn, and they have already done much to improve the furnishings of the Cathedral.

Court of Charles II at Winchester THE ancient city of Winchester presented a lively appearance that summer morning in the year of grace, 1683, when the travellers, whose adventures we are going to recount, awoke in their vast four-post beds and looked from the windows of the George Inn on to the busy scene below.

The windows of High Street, which they had seen on their arrival on the previous night, illuminated with coloured lamps, were now gay with flags and flowers in honour of the King's presence there with his Court. Festoons were looped over the street from one side to the other, and were reflected in the foaming torrent that flowed down the middle, bearing the city's refuse to the Itchen. High Street presented a very picturesque appearance that morning. Its houses were chiefly built in the quaint timbered style of a century before, and their sharp pointed gables contrasted oddly with the more solid red-brick houses of the day. At the far end of the street the squalid huts of the poor clustered round the grey East Gate, while St. Giles' Hill, then a fine

STUART
WINCHESTER
AS IT MIGHT HAVE BEEN
according to
the Plans of
WREN

C.G STEVENS
Delt 1921

SOUTHGATE   C H A R L E S   II^s   P A L A C E   WESTGATE
          C A T H E D R A L   S^T THOMAS' CHURCH   HIGH STREET

piece of unspoilt down, rose above all. Nearer at hand rose West Gate, where debtors were imprisoned in a noisome hole, begging their food through a hole in the floor.

Presently Sir Marmaduke and Lady Banks, for such we will suppose the name of our travellers to have been, crossed the High Street with some difficulty, as the latter did not like to wet her trailing skirts in the foaming drain. Safely over, however, they passed the City Cross and tower of St. Lawrence, and came into the Square, then the city market-place. Here a scene of great beauty met their eyes. The busy booths of the market with their bright awnings were grouped round an irregular space, and above the busy hum of the purchasers' chatter rose the shrill cries of the sellers who thus tried to attract their attention. Among the gaily attired throng, the brilliant uniforms of the King's new guards glowed here and there, the whole like a kaleidoscope against a background of fragrant lime trees on either side of the avenue leading to the Cathedral west front. Underneath the ponderous walls of the great Church, and resembling nothing so much as butterflies, flitted the lords and ladies of the Merry Monarch's court, the former in great black periwigs with feathered hats and much brocade and lace, the latter in light and graceful summer dresses, with their own curls beneath shady hats.

Here and there a clergyman in sombre black with wide hat, snuff-coloured wig and snowy lappets, walked pompously to and fro. Beside the Churchyard gate sat unnoticed an aged apple-woman, who had lost all her relations in the Great Plague that had devastated Winchester some years before. Suddenly a vision of lace and beauty, who had entered the market, approached her, and with a few words of sympathy, pressed enough money to keep her for a year into her hand, and flitted away without waiting for thanks.

On asking who she might be, our travellers learnt to their astonishment that this was Nell Gwynn on her way to see the King from her house in St. Peter Street (if it was in St. Peter Street, for many houses claim the honour of lodging her). She always pitied the poor, did Nell, they were told. It was she who had persuaded Charles to build Chelsea Hospital ; and, after all, she was an orange-girl herself once.

Sir Marmaduke and Lady Banks now proceeded into the Close, and as they approached the Deanery a strange company came out.

A little bowing figure, in black clerical costume, was backing out through the three-arched porch of the building. With several men and the fair Nell Gwynn, all in fits of laughter, came a tall saturnine man with black eyebrows, eyes, and wig, and, striving to conceal his amusement, he helped the Dean (for it was he) to his feet as he nearly tripped over the step. His Majesty King Charles II (known to his intimates as Old Rowley), whom our friends had immediately recognised in the tall and dissipated-looking gentleman, was surrounded by spaniels, while two more were in his arms and one on his shoulders. At the King's side walked a man of middle height with an enormous sandy wig, his eyebrows slightly raised, and an expression of amused contempt on his handsome features. This was Baptist May, " the wickedest man," says Pepys, " that I ever knew," which is not surprising when we learn he was the keeper of Charles's morals. He swept off his plumed hat to the cheering crowd, and, encumbered as he was, advanced to meet two men approaching from the Close Gate.

These were the gorgeously dressed Duke of Buckingham, a stout red-faced gentleman, one of the King's greatest friends, and with him a man of harsh and austere countenance, also in the height of fashion, who looked with displeasure at the King, and observed how unsafe it was for him to walk about unguarded. "Never fear, brother James," rejoined the King, "they'll never kill me to make you King." Meanwhile the venerable bowed figure of Bishop Morley was seen approaching through the Deanery garden, past the new wing of bright-red brick which had been built on for the King's use. With him was a sharp-faced little man, with fine eyes, Thomas Ken ; and his well-known friend Izaak Walton, with a fishing rod over his shoulder. After speaking with the King for a minute or two, Walton observed that sorry as he was to leave the Royal presence for such a sordid occupation, he must really go in search for brandlings, "little red worms" as he explained "to be found on an old dunghill or some very rotten place near it," else he should catch no skeggars that day. So he walked off down Dome Alley to the red-gabled house, now called No. 7 The Close, where he dwelt with his son-in-law the Canon.

Meanwhile Prebendary Ken had departed on his way to the Cathedral door. Under his arm was a little volume of hymns and devotions devised by himself for the use of the Winchester scholars. As he passed the company lapsed into silence, none wishing to provoke the Prebendary's tongue, for he was wont, in practice as in precept, to speak his mind and " in conversation be sincere."

Suddenly a fussy little man in maroon velvet appeared round the corner, running very fast, his gigantic wig all awry, his face purple with exertion, and his arms full of flapping papers that dropped as he ran. Charles burst into uproarious laughter, and even the Duke of York's harsh features relaxed into an unwilling smile.

Meanwhile the irate little man, who had lost his temper with his breath, was being besieged by the mild Bishop Morley and the Headmaster of Winchester College, who addressed him as Dr. Wren, and who without any effect plied him with questions about the two buildings, Wolvesey and School respectively, in which they were interested. Charles, however, now came up, and with exquisite tact smoothed the ruffled feathers of the architect, and an eager discussion about the new Palace and its marble staircase arose. They could see it from where they stood, a great red pile on the hill west of the Cathedral, destined to be left unfinished.

Soon the merry company moved on to a bowling green near the west front and jested as they played. And meanwhile the unhappy Queen sat in her little house in Canon Street—alone.

Three years later, Charles was dead, and James was King, Catherine was a widow, and Winchester a forgotten provincial town.

St. Cross.

THE " Hospital " of St. Cross enters little into the history of the City : yet it is an architectural monument of such extreme interest that it has a right to be treated at length. It has, therefore, been made the subject of a separate chapter.

Henry de Blois

In 1136 that great and ambitious statesman-bishop, Henry de Blois, brother of Stephen, the reigning King, founded the Hospital of St. Cross, nearly a mile outside the city walls. It is not easy to account for its position. A Latin record may throw a little light, and we give it for what it is worth :—*In loco ubi nescio quid coenoboli ante aliquot saecula positum sed a Danis dirutum et destructum fuerat.* So St. Cross may mark the site of an earlier Saxon convent. At any rate, it was suitably situated for the Knights of St. John of Jerusalem. Here, hard by the Southampton Road, they could hear their last Mass before passing down to the port, and taking ship to the land of the Holy Cross itself. Pilgrims on their way from Southampton to Canterbury also stopped to hear Mass at St. Cross. The Chapel used both by them and the Knights of St. John was dedicated to St. Thomas of Canterbury, and is now behind the organ. The charter that put the Knights in charge of St. Cross was confirmed in 1151, providing amongst other things for the maintenance and housing of " thirteen poor, impotent men "—a number that has never been diminished ; the brethren of this foundation still wear the distinctive mark of the long black gown and the silver cross. As soon, however, as

1185 the Knights of St. John were behaving badly, and, only thirty-four years after the granting of the Charter, Bishop Toclyve was beseeching the Papal Legate to force the Knights to surrender St. Cross. The Legate attempted to do so, but he and the Bishop were severely snubbed two years later, when the Pope reinstated the Knights. But their triumph was short-lived. In 1203 they lost their hold on St. Cross for good and all.

The building of the Church had meanwhile **The Church** reached completion. The western part of the Nave cannot indeed (if we may judge by its pointed windows of the Early English type) have been finished very much before 1200. The other buildings seem to have lain to the south (as is usual in monastic buildings), and not, as they now do, to the north of the Church. But neither Church nor dwelling-houses were destined to remain in their original state. Towards 1350 William of Edyngton, then Master of St. Cross and Rector of Cheriton (a combination of functions which occurs more than once), shewed great energy in performing his duties, in fact his zeal earned his promotion to the episcopal chair of Winchester. He has left his mark on St. Cross: for he probably completed the clerestory of the Nave, and the roof, which heretofore had been thatched, he covered with lead.

Wykeham, who succeeded to the bishopric on **Wykeham** Edyngton's death, was early interested in St. Cross. As a boy at the City Grammar School, he had enjoyed along with the others the privilege of wandering through its close, and even receiving the hospitality of the Brethren in the great Hall. When he became Bishop he showed his interest by appointing to the Mastership the most capable man he knew, one John de Campeden, under

143

whose guiding hand the Hospital recovered something of its lost glory. To John, dying in 1410, there was set up a fine memorial, a great brass still to be seen within the altar rails.

Beaufort After John's death the place declined once more, until Beaufort founded it afresh. Its new charter gave provision for "a warden, two priests, thirty-five brethren, and two sisters, who are to tend them in times of sickness." To this day these Brethren of Beaufort's foundation wear the distinguishing red or plum-coloured gowns with the Cardinal's badge and hat on a silver plate. To provide the necessary funds for this new establishment Beaufort gave St. Cross the revenues of the parish church of St. Faith, which once stood at the junction of Kingsgate Road and the Southampton Road, now marked by the graveyard only. St. Faith's was demolished in the sixteenth century, and part of its stone screen may be seen in the chancel of St. Cross.

Beaufort went further, and prepared plans for the complete transformation of the Hospital. In 1447, however, only eight or nine months after he had obtained his charter to build, he passed away and was buried in his beautiful Chapel in Cathedral. That being so, he can hardly have witnessed the building of the Great Hall, the houses of the brethren with their tall chimneys, and the so-called Beaufort tower over the gate-way, all of which are normally ascribed to him ; they were no doubt built from money which he left for the purpose, and from designs of which he had approved.

The Reformation and after At the time of the Dissolution the Foundation escaped fairly lightly, and the Mastership was still a coveted post. Lord Brooke, in 1603, had been hoping to get it, and when he failed, it is said he joined the Bye Plot from sheer disappointment. At his execution at Winchester they arranged as a grim joke that he should see the tower of the Church from the scaffold ; and at the sight, they say, the poor man finally broke down.

Amongst the many men who held the position Lord Brooke had so coveted, comes one John Cooke, whose name appears among those that condemned King Charles to death—this fellow met with his deserts when Charles II came by his own.

In 1848 a Chancery suit was instituted against the then Master, Francis North, Earl of Guildford, who was accused of mismanagement. The suit continued till 1853, and cost £5,600. It formed the original for Anthony Trollope's novel *The Warden*. The case resulted in the present scheme under which the Hospital is administered by a Board of Trustees, of whom the Master is one. Since this fundamental change there have been few events of note in the history of the Hospital. At present the number of brethren supported is eighteen of De Blois Foundation (black) and nine of Beaufort's (red) ; there are also numerous out-patients.

The building begun by Henry de Blois was **The Church** not finished until the end of the thirteenth century. The Church starts at the east end by being Norman, and ends at the west in the Gothic style. The three western bays of the Abbey Church at Romsey provide a still finer instance of this transition from Norman to Gothic.

The main features of the Church have, how- **Exterior** ever, nothing of the true Gothic. Weight is here carried not by the aid of counteracting buttress, and neatly balanced arch-thrusts, but by mere

145   L

thickness of walls and strength of ponderous columns. It is heavy and dour, but there is something satisfactory in its heaviness. It stands for strength and endurance. Externally it resembles a fortress.

Upon the east rise two Norman pinnacles like turrets. What external decoration it possesses has been put upon the north side. It is conjectured that since the secular buildings were on the south, the north alone was visible as a visitor approached. Lastly, there is the curious triple Norman arch in the angle of the south transept and the choir which is without parallel.

Interior Within, we find the choir and transepts of highly finished late Norman. The pointed arch is already creeping in, but it is noticeable that it is used only where weight has to be borne, as in the chancel and aisle vaults and arcades. The windows, on the other hand, where decoration and not construction has to be thought of, are still round-headed. The decoration is lavish. In the north transept is a famous window fringed with a border of birds, all stretching their beaks towards the same centre. The old Norman interior was, of course, painted ; at St. Albans, indeed, some of the original colour remains. In about 1880 Mr. Butterfield, a celebrated architect, supervised the redecoration of the choir with colour in the mediaeval style. This innovation was more criticised than approved, and in 1927 the decoration was entirely removed.

De Blois' work was long in getting done, for the country was in an unsettled state. This delay in completion makes the Nave the most interesting part of the Church. The massive columns are typical of the strength of twelfth century masonry. Their circumference exceeds their height by three feet! The stone bases on which they stand are both effective and unusual. The roof rose from immediately above the arches, and was thatched. The aisle walls were the last part finished, it would seem, for one can trace the progress of the styles as it develops from east to west. On the south side of the Nave (exterior) are three windows : the first round-headed and quite plain ; the second is still round, but has a hood moulding ; the third and most western window is typical early Gothic, with hood moulding, pointed arch, and flanking pilasters all complete. To these three stages in the windows answer three similar stages in the buttresses. The earliest and most eastern is merely a thickening of the wall ; the second protrudes slightly from the wall, and has a single set-off or step in it ; the third projects further still, and has two sets-off. See Diagram, p. 199

The west window is a magnificent example of Decorated work, the finest in Winchester. Of the same date are the door below it and the north porch. The Nave clerestory was added in the same style, but later, just before Perpendicular set in. It is worth noting a point or two of special interest within the Nave. A stone bracket on the second pillar of the Nave (counting from the east) once held the Holy Cross, and it was so contrived that about Easter the rising sun fell through the transept window upon the bracket and its Cross. Two specimens of late fifteenth century glass remained in the western windows of the clerestory on either side, but have now been moved to where they can be seen more easily.

Of the brasses in St. Cross Church the most important is that of John de Campeden. It lies at the foot of the altar steps, immediately within **Campeden's Brass** the rails, and is in beautiful preservation, only a small portion near the right foot being lost. Though John de Campeden did not die until 1410, the brass appears to have been executed about 1382, probably, as was the frequent custom, under his own supervision. He is shewn in full processional vestments, and the orphreys of his cope are embroidered within alternate suns and lions' heads. The effigy measures six feet in length, and is a superb example of the best period of brass engraving. The other two brasses, on each side of the Chancel within the rails, represent Thomas Lawne (1518), Rector of Mottisfont, in Mass vestments, and Richard Halkard, " Warden of this Hospital " (1493), in processional vestments without the cope. He wears the low-pointed Doctor's cap. Both are good examples of their period, and are preserved entire.

Beaufort's Buildings

The secular buildings were built by the order and from the plans of Cardinal Beaufort.

On entering the Beaufort gate we have the great Hall on our right. Here on great days the Brethren dine. It is a spacious room with traceried windows. At one end is a staircase to the room above the tower. The Cardinal's chair stands on the daïs, and is not so uncomfortable as it looks. In a case near by is an unique coin : it was struck by Beaufort with his own device upon it—a remarkable testimony to the power of the man that he should dare to mint his own coinage.

Passing along a passage we reach the kitchen, with a great fireplace, and arrangements for turning the spit by the aid of the smoke. Now it is only used on those rare occasions when the Brethren dine together in the Hall.

So have the great men of Winchester shown their care for the aged. Though it is linked with the high-sounding names of Beaufort and de Blois, it is not the burying ground of heroes, but of gentle, kind, old men. It boasts no pompous monuments or regimental banners, but simple epitaphs to de Campeden, Peter de Sancta Maria, and such godly men.

Winchester College, 1394—1933.

On Saturday, March 28th, 1394,* "the first entrance of the Warden, Fellows, Scholars, and all the rest aforesaid, took place at the third hour before noon, walking in procession, preceded by the cross erect."

*   *   *   *   *

Unsettled
State of
England at
the time
of the
Foundation

The Middle Ages had still a hundred years to run, judged by our arbitrary standards of time, but the new wine had already begun to ferment in the old bottles. It was a restless and questioning time. The Catholic Church was still supreme in the kingdoms of Europe and in the minds of men : but she had long since left behind the spiritual glories of St. Francis and the temporal glories of Innocent III, and was falling gradually into the slow decline that ended in the Protestant schism. English politics and English society were unsettled and confused. Feudal organisation—never as complete in this country as on the Continent—was beginning to break up, and in the process many ancient landmarks were disappearing. Everything was fluid and unstable, both in Church and State. When Wykeham reached the height of his wealth and fame, Edward III, once a great conqueror and a great legislator, was sinking into a lecherous old age, while rival barons harried the peace of the kingdom. In 1380, only fourteen years before the foundation of Winchester, Wycliffe had issued

* Mr. Leach (*History of Winchester College*, p. 129) has shown that 1394 was the correct date, not 1393. Heete, from whose account the above is taken, was also mistaken in including the Fellows in this solemn procession. They did not appear till later in that year.

from Oxford a denial of the cardinal doctrine of Transubstantiation and for the next fifteen years the Lollard missionaries, who drew their inspiration from him, were travelling about in the Midlands, in the West and round London, preaching doctrines subversive in the highest degree of current theology and established ecclesiastical order. A year later, in 1381, came the Peasants' Revolt, and for a moment the whole structure of society seemed to be tottering. In the world of affairs Parliament was beginning to feel its strength : but it was without experience and had as yet no unity of purpose. What was gained one session was lost the next. John of Gaunt and, when his day had passed, the favourites of Richard II were the real masters of England. The seeds of our civil liberties were being quietly sown : but the nobles had to exterminate each other in the Wars of the Roses and our polity to submit to Tudor discipline, before that seed could come to harvest.

Twice in these tumultuous years the Founder was called to the first place in the Government. Everything we know about him—and his portrait also—suggests that he was a conciliator and a friend of peace, anxious to win the confidence of both parties. He was probably not a great minister, though he seems to have recognised constitutional principles and to have sided, so far as he took sides at all, with the popular party. Perhaps we may describe him best as a typical fourteenth century civil servant : a capable administrator, cautious and reasonable, entirely satisfied with the traditions and opinions of his circle, and, though not harsh with heretics and revolutionaries, yet possessed with a deep affection for the old order in Church and State and anxious to maintain it. Moreover, though not a great theologian or a great ecclesiastic, he was a man pious after the piety of his age. The sense of sin was strong in the mediaeval mind. The frescoes in the Campo Santo at Pisa, to take one example out of many, show how terrible were the visions of future retribution that haunted the imaginations of men : and in Purgatory they conceived the dead to be suffering similar pains, though lighter and not unending. These pains could be lessened by prayers and especially masses offered by the living. Hence the foundation of numerous chantry-chapels in the 14th and 15th centuries, and the special provision made for the daily singing of masses in them for the souls of their founders and those to whom their founders owed some obligation. Wykeham attached very great importance to these observances ; we still have the agreement drawn up between him and the Prior of St. Swithun's, stipulating for the singing of several masses each day in his chapel in Cathedral for the souls of himself and his parents. It is carefully provided that if the priest, whose usual duty it is to officiate at these masses, falls suddenly ill, the Prior is at once to appoint another to take his place, so that the daily stream of intercession may never fail.

His Object in founding College
With these two ideas foremost in his mind— to secure the peace of his soul and to strengthen the position of his Church—Wykeham looked about him for some fitting object upon which to employ his great wealth. (In 1535 the revenues of the See of Winchester were estimated at £60,000 a year in modern values.) Two hundred years earlier he might have built a monastery : but at the end of the fourteenth century monasteries were losing favour not only with the

people at large, but also with the secular clergy, who looked jealously upon their numerous privileges and exemptions. Besides, if the Church was to be defended from her enemies, her champions must be men of the world, not shut up in a cloister. Champions she must have, if she was to retain her property, her pre-eminence in government and her hold over the popular mind : and among those champions there must be theologians able to refute Wycliffe, and lawyers able to rise, as Wykeham had risen, to the right hand of the throne. Here their trained intellects would be at the service of the State, no doubt, in the performance both of its executive and judicial functions : but they would also form a solid phalanx in defence of the wealth and privileges of their Church, threatened then from two opposite quarters—by John of Gaunt and the nobles as well as by the villeins who laboured resentfully on her great estates.

Everything then pointed to an educational **Need for** foundation of some kind. He himself was **Education** without a complete education and consequently **among** was able to appreciate its value. He may have **the Clergy** had the penetration to see that the Lollards could never be conquered by persecution : they must be beaten, if they could be beaten, by superior learning and superior example, and this learning and this example the priests of his own day could not show. In 1387 he severely rebuked the Prior of St. Swithun for the ignorance of the monks and its discreditable results : "not understanding what they read, but being almost wholly ignorant of letters, in singing and reading they often put a short accent for a long and contrariwise : and walking in the wilderness out of the way defile and pervert the sound meaning of the

Scriptures " : and he gave instructions that a master should be appointed to teach the novices grammar. This no doubt was a common state of affairs : and the need for a new order of priests had been accentuated by the Black Death, which fell upon the country in 1349, carrying away between a third and a half of the whole population, including a very large proportion of the parish clergy. The wastage had to be made good : and the Founder perceived that he could render no greater service than by helping to fill the gap. He would devote his riches to providing that the recruits should be fit men, living under discipline in magnificent homes, relieved from material cares, trained in the full cycle of mediaeval study and steeped at their most impressionable age in that tradition of godliness and good learning to which he looked for the salvation of his Church.

The idea was not a new one and in its execution Wykeham generally followed precedent, except in the scale of his design, which far surpassed anything previously attempted. Four of his predecessors in the royal service—Walter de Merton, Bishop of Rochester, the founder of Merton : Walter de Stapledon, Bishop of Exeter, the founder of Exeter : Robert de Egglesfield, the founder of Queen's : and Adam de Brome, the founder of Oriel—had used their wealth to make provision for the comfort and discipline of the thousands of needy students who thronged the lecture rooms of Oxford. But the number of scholars to be housed in New College alone—seventy—nearly equalled the number at all the other colleges together and the endowment did actually exceed all theirs. It was not without hesitation that he took his decision. He tells us in his own words that he debated long within himself whether it would not be better to distribute all his goods to the poor and leave no foundation : he had seen so many instances of benefactors' intentions perverted and their liberality abused. But having once made up his mind, he gave with both hands :—" To their (the poor scholars') help and relief we have finally bent the shoulders of compassion and are prepared for this to spend all our wealth and work . . . . that so the praise of God may be spread, the Church ruled, the strength and fervour of the Christian religion grow hotter and all knowledge and virtue be increased in strength."

The design was carried out much as it had originally taken shape in the Founder's mind. From the first it was his intention to found two Colleges, one at Oxford and the other at Winchester, each standing in the closest connection with the other and the latter supplying the former with a steady stream of students. The two Colleges " issue from one stem and flow from one spring and differ not in substance having no diverse effect." Each was necessary to the other. The scholars of " Our College at Oxford " were to study theology, civil and canon law, and philosophy : but before any real progress could be made in the higher branches of learning, it was essential that the foundations should be well and truly laid—"As experience, the mistress of life, teaches, grammar is the foundation, gate and source of all the liberal arts, without which they cannot be known, nor can anyone arrive at their pursuit . . . . and some students of other sciences, through default of good and sufficient teaching in Latin, deficient in grammar, often fall into danger." (Foundation Deed, 1382.) The Founder had here detected perhaps the most serious weakness in fourteenth century education. " Latin was nowhere studied or taught with any thoroughness. In the north of Europe especially it was all but ignored in the University schools." Boys came to the University at the age of 14 or so, without a proper grounding in the elements, and naturally quite unfitted to grapple with the difficulties of the Latin Aristotle and the other text-books of scholasticism. Wykeham resolved that his scholars should not proceed to the higher studies until they had acquired a sound and scholarly knowledge of Grammar, which meant " the study of language and of literature, more especially of the Latin speech and writers." They were accordingly to remain at Winchester till they were 16 and to pass thence to New College as vacancies arose. None but Wykehamists could obtain entry into New College : the election *ad Winton* as well as *ad Oxon* was to be in the hands of a joint board consisting of the two Wardens, two Fellows of New College, and the Sub-Warden and the Headmaster of Winchester.

Foundation of New College
The Founder was appointed Bishop of Winchester in 1366. In 1369 he began to buy land in Oxford ; the foundation charter of New College was issued in 1379, and on April 14th, 1386, the Society entered its new home. Temporary arrangements had already been made at Winchester. In 1373 Wykeham entered into an agreement with Master Richard Herton, *grammaticus*, that the latter should for ten years instruct in the art of grammar " the seventy scholars whom the Bishop maintains and will maintain at his own cost." The progress of the

work was interrupted in 1376, when Wykeham was deprived of the temporalities of his See : they were restored to him the year after and in 1382 the foundation deed was executed.

The College at Winchester was to consist of a Warden, a Headmaster, ten Fellows, three Chaplains, an Usher, seventy Scholars, three Clerks to sing in Chapel, sixteen Quiristers and a large staff of servants. The Fellows, as we have seen, did not appear till late in 1394 : but the provision made for them illustrates clearly the double function which the Founder intended the College to perform. It was to be a Collegiate Church, that is to say, a Church served by a college of priests, with duties similar to those of a Cathedral Chapter, but ranking below them in dignity. It would be the task of these priests to maintain the frequent and elaborate services in Chapel and to offer daily for the soul of the Founder those prayers which he valued so highly. To this Collegiate Church was to be attached, in accordance with a common practice in the Middle Ages, a Grammar School, in which the seventy were to be taught. The College was thus to be a Chantry as well as a School : the two functions were to be kept distinct and probably as much importance was attached to the one as to the other. It is not a legitimate use of language to say that Wykeham founded the English Public School. The expression " Public School " has come now to mean almost the precise opposite of what it originally signified. Public Schools, strictly speaking, were schools governed by guilds or municipalities, and there were numbers of these in all parts of England before Wykeham's time. We have Municipal Schools to-day, but a distinction is drawn between them and the Public

Schools. If words are to mean what they say, the great Public Schools of to-day should be called the great Private Schools. Nothing corresponding to our idea of a Public School was ever present in Wykeham's mind. Winchester is merely the doyen of the group of schools to which the Legislature from accidental causes has given the name Public.

Revenues The College was endowed with estates in Wiltshire and Hampshire (in the neighbourhood of Southampton and Andover), together with certain manors in the Thames Valley, near Twickenham. Due care was taken to obtain from the King a charter of privileges, exempting the College property from the payment of the customary aids and services. The total income from endowments reached about £450 at the outset (*i.e.*, approximately £9000 of our money) —barely sufficient to maintain the Society.

Buildings The fabric was six years in building and a sum of £1014. 8s. 3d. (about £20,000 of our money) was spent upon it. The site was bounded on the north by the Priory of St. Swithun and Wykeham's palace of Wolvesey, on the east by Bishop Pontissara's College of St. Elizabeth, which stood where the Warden's kitchen garden is now ; on the south by the gardens of the Carmelite Friars, which stretched to a line drawn roughly south-east from Darius Corner across to Meads Wall ; and on the west by the Sustern Spital or Sisters' Hospital, which stood where Moberly Library stands now. There were no Meads till 1544, when the Carmelite gardens passed to the College under an exchange with the Crown, and it was not until the Wardenship of Huntingford (1789—1832) that they became fully available for the Scholars.

It used to be thought that Wykeham himself drew the plans of his College : and support was added to this belief by the undoubted fact that he served for several years as *supervisor* of the King's works at Windsor and elsewhere. The meaning of this word is open to doubt : but on comparing its use in other cases and its application to other persons, it appears likely that the duties assigned to a *supervisor* were rather to obtain labour and material than to draw the plans. The architect was very possibly William Winford, who was appointed under Wykeham's Will to carry out alterations in the nave of Cathedral, and whose portrait is to be seen under the head of Jesse in the east window of Chapel.

As at New College, the exterior is bare and **Outer Court** unadorned, testifying to the turbulence of the times. The rising of 1381 had witnessed a number of attacks upon religious houses, and if the beauties within were to be preserved from damage, the walls must be strong and able to withstand assault. But the austerity of the front was partly relieved by the beautiful Madonna statue over Outer Gate. Curiously enough, this figure has only recently attracted the attention of historians and critics : but they do not hesitate to call it one of the masterpieces of mediaeval English sculpture. Outer Court was surrounded by various offices : the Steward's chamber was placed over the gate, where it has remained ever since, while to the east of the gate were granaries, and to the west a brewery and a slaughter-house. It was not until the early seventeenth century that the proportions of Outer Court were marred by the encroachments of the Warden's house : and the screen at the western end was not built till 1663.

Chamber Court remains much as it was, except that windows have been opened looking inwards in the second storey. The ground-floor chambers were occupied by the scholars, with the exception of Seventh, which was the schoolroom—the oldest in England—and the room to the west of Sixth (now forming part of Thule chamber) into which were packed the sixteen quiristers. The two upstairs chambers on the east side of Chamber Court and " Ken " were reserved for the Fellows, three in each. Election Chamber and the room above were set apart for the Warden's lodgings, and what is now the Second Master's study was until 1730 reserved for the Warden of New College : the dining room in the Second Master's house was occupied by the Headmaster, the Usher and the remaining Fellow : and the drawing room by the three Chaplains. How and when the buildings adjoining the Second Master's house on the west came to be there has not been ascertained. The ground floor space west of the quiristers' chamber was originally occupied by a bakehouse, and we know that a Mr. Dobins, who was elected Fellow in 1585, made some additions to that corner of the fabric. The room now occupied by College Tutor was formerly a Fellows' Common Room.

On the west side of Chamber Court, adjoining the Chaplains' room, was the kitchen. Then as now it ran the whole height of the buildings, and originally comprised organ room and the lobby beneath it, which did not attain to a separate existence till sometime in the sixteenth century. The Trusty Servant is the work of a scholar named John Hoskyns and dates from the early part of the seventeenth century. He is supposed to have been put into Windsor

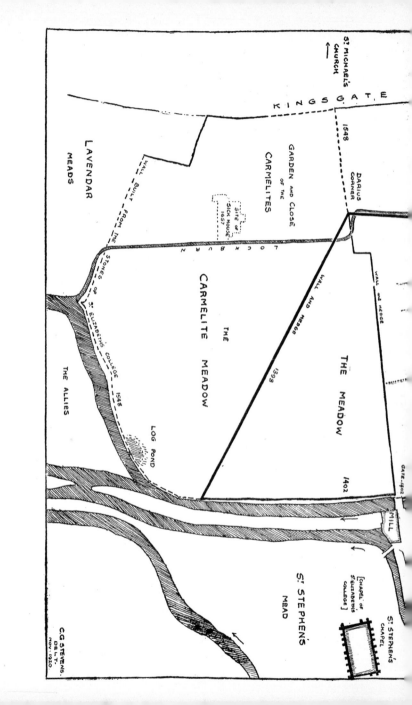

interior is slowly resuming its proper
ty.

e original tower was a circular structure
unted by a spire. It was rebuilt by Warden
between 1474 and 1480 in something
aching its present form, and at the same
Thurbern's Chantry was rebuilt at the
-west corner of Chapel, thus forming a basis
support for the tower. Thurbern was
den from 1413 to 1450 and left property to
College for the celebration of his *obit*. The
r became seriously insecure in the middle of
last century and in 1863 was taken down,
re-erected on a concrete foundation to the
ory of Warden Williams of New College and
den Barter of Winchester.

oisters are part of the original fabric. They
used as a burial ground for Fellows (a
ial Bull of privilege being obtained from the
e for that purpose), as a summer schoolroom,
also perhaps for processions on feast-days,
New College—" circa claustrum processiones
solennes." Chantry was completed about
by the executors of John Fromond, steward
the Wiltshire and Hampshire manors, who
property to the College for the singing of the
tomary masses for his soul. It fell into disuse
he sixteenth century, when the chantries were
pressed by Act of Parliament under Edward VI,
from 1629 to 1875 was used as a Library for
Fellows. In 1875 by a happy conversion it
ame a chapel for juniors. The ancient glass
w in the east window of Chantry dates from
ut 1480. It originally formed part of the
zing of Thurbern's Chantry, and was moved
its present position in 1772. Of the original
antry glass, which was the work of John Prudde

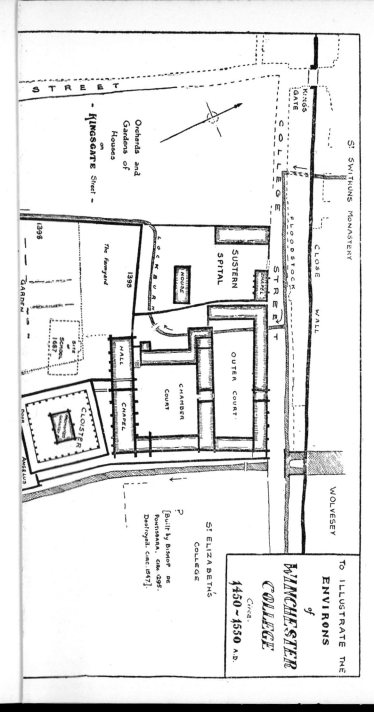

TO ILLUSTRATE THE
ENVIRONS
of
WINCHESTER
COLLEGE
Circa.
1450~1550 A.D.

uniform in hono
College.

The line of Hal
but there have be
was originally ado⟩
and there was no
sixteenth century.
is the earliest in ⟨
1596. The large ⟨
beautiful indeed.

The interior of
the hands of refo⟩
still admire, as Wa⟩
fifteenth century, t⟩
proportions : but
aspect have been
Chapel was originall⟩
screen, which ran ε
The walls were cov
the altar were gorge⟨
were filled with stai⟩
judge from the thre
Kensington, must ha⟩
richness of colour.
of his glass and his ⟩
to in the Statutes, an⟩
damage or break the⟩
gone the hangings an⟩
all—scattered and fo⟩
beautiful glass. Of t⟩
of oak stalls with th⟩
side of the choir is
original splendours ⟨
the Reformation a⟩
were undertaken by
His wainscoting was
now at last after seve⟩

**Cower and
Churbern's
Chantry**

Cloisters

Chantry

the
digni⟩
Th⟩
surm⟩
Bake⟩
appr⟨
time
soutl⟩
and
War⟨
the ⟨
towe⟩
the
and
mem⟩
War⟩
C⟨
wer⟨
spe⟨
Pop⟩
and⟩
as a⟩
fian⟩
144⟩
of
left⟩
cus⟩
in t⟩
sup⟩
an⟩
the⟩
be⟨
no⟩
ab⟨
gla⟩
to
Ch⟩

of Westminster, King's glasier to Henry VI, only a few fragments remain. The upper storey of this beautiful little building formerly housed the Fellows' Library but it has recently been turned into a Drawing School. It is a room almost perfectly suited to this purpose, being both light and very quiet.

Before passing to the history of the College we The Statutes must devote a few words to the Statutes. They were drawn up by Wykeham with the utmost care, being revised and added to probably three times before the final and authoritative edition was issued in 1400. His experience as an administrator and a judge had accustomed him to the making and interpretation of rules, and in the Statutes of Winchester we find every detail of the Society's life regulated with minute precision. Substantial parts of the code were taken from the statutes of previous Founders : and in their turn they became a model for later ages. The principal and most famous provisions are that the scholars shall be *pauperes et indigentes* (Rubric II) : that in addition to the seventy there may be taken into the College at their own expense *pensionarii*, sons of influential and well-disposed persons—the germ of Commoners (Rubric XVI) : and that in each of the six chambers there are to be three of the elder and discreeter scholars chosen to superintend the behaviour and studies of their juniors— a provision taken from the Statutes of Merton and surviving to the present day in many types of school in all lands (Rubric XXXIV). Special concessions are introduced for the benefit of Founder's kin : they may stay from 7 to 25 and the standard of attainment required of them on admission need not be so high as with the rest. A strong monastic strain runs through the code.

163

No boy is to be admitted who is suffering from any incurable defect which would disqualify him for Holy Orders. The services in Chapel are regulated in detail : every scholar by the end of his first year must have received the first tonsure : and on no account is any woman to enter the precincts. Clothes for the wash are to be handed to a *lotrix* of approved character at the gate. There is to be no waste : the number of horses in the retinue of the Warden of New College when he comes with the posers to hold an election is carefully prescribed : the daily allowance of food and the yearly allowance of cloth for gowns is specified. No dogs, hawks or ferrets are to be kept in the College : sowers of discord are to have their commons stopped : and there is to be no wrestling or throwing of balls in Chapel or Hall or upsetting of beer and other liquids. But his administrative wisdom failed him in one particular. Thinking no doubt of the abuses he had discovered at St. Cross in the early years of his Episcopate, Wykeham sought to bind the College for ever in obedience to his Statutes and his only, without power of amendment or repeal. They began to grow obsolete within a hundred and fifty years : yet they remained in operation for a good three hundred years more, distorted, as we shall see, and betrayed by those who professed to be their stoutest champions. Their story might have afforded Carlyle with another example of an attempt " to chain the Future under the Past . . . . A wholly insane attempt ; and for man himself, could it prosper, the frightfullest of all enchantments, a very Life-in-Death."

We have dwelt thus at length on the circumstances and incidents of the foundation because it is by far the most important event in the history of the College. In a sense we have not and were not intended to have a history : it was the Founder's desire that these two Societies should live on quietly from century to century under an unalterable code, discharging without interruption their double duty of prayer and study. That intention has in the main been carried out, and consequently our history is lacking in incident. The first century witnessed a fertilising extension of Wykehamist influence through various channels in many different fields. The next two hundred years bring us into touch with national history at several points : but there was no break in the continuity of our work. Then followed a century and a half of eclipse, dating roughly from the death of Warden Harris in 1658 to the election of Warden Barter in 1832. The fetters of the past lay heavy on us and the obligations of the trust were forgotten. It was not until the forties and fifties of the last century that the tide of reform reached our walls : but though it came late, it came in strength. Both the Colleges at length surrendered themselves to it and their tradition revived at once in all its ancient strength.

We shall touch briefly on each of these periods in turn, noticing at the same time the names and careers of our most famous men.

The books of the steward of Hall show plainly, from the number of guests whose presence is recorded in them, that the opening of the College aroused a wide interest : the King himself (Henry IV) came to visit it in 1399. It seems to have taken rank at once as the first foundation of its kind in the land : and the sumptuous scale on which it was planned, and the ability of our early Headmasters, made it at once a model and a reservoir for later founders. Among the probationary Fellows in residence at New College in the first year of its existence was Henry Chicheley, Archbishop of Canterbury, and the War Minister of Agincourt, the prelate into whose mouth Shakespeare put the speech about the honey bees in Henry V. Following Wykeham's example he established two Colleges, one at his native place, Higham Ferrers, and the other, All Souls at Oxford. The model afforded by the statutes and design of New College was very closely followed, though the scale of the foundation was smaller. But the most conspicuous of our early imitators was Henry VI. From his cradle he had Wykehamists round him : Chicheley was his godfather and Bekington, Bishop of Bath and Wells, his tutor ; and when he started to plan his own foundations of Eton and King's College, Cambridge, it was to Winchester and New College that he looked for examples and advisers. He frequently visited Winchester and gave the College noble gifts. The design of the royal foundations and the relations of the two Colleges to each other are reproduced from Wykeham's scheme. The Headmaster of Winchester, William Waynflete, and at least six of his scholars were removed to Eton in 1442 to give the sister-foundation a fair start : the cloth for the Eton gowns was bought at Winchester and it stands recorded in our accounts that five men were employed to convey to Eton a specimen of the ground upon which Winchester stood, perhaps that it might impart some native Wykehamist virtue to the Etonian atmosphere. Of the first five Headmasters of Eton, four were Wykehamists. On July 1st, 1448, the alliance received formal sanction : the two Colleges of St. Mary Winton and the two Royal Colleges of Eton and Cambridge

Chicheley and All Souls

Henry VI

Foundation of Eton

entered into the *Amicabilis Concordia*, of which a copy hangs in Moberly Library, for mutual support in all quarrels and suits at law.

Waynflete holds a place in English educational history almost as important as that of Wykeham. He passed in 1447 from the Provostship of Eton to the Bishopric of Winchester and in the following year the foundation charter of Magdalen College was issued. Like All Souls it is the manifest daughter of New College and its first President was a Wykehamist. Three schools were established in connection with Magdalen, the College School at Oxford and two others at Wainfleet and Brackley. The Oxford school represented in one respect a wholly new departure : its pupils were to receive instruction in " grammar, poems and other arts of *humanitas*," a clear indication that the advanced guards of Renaissance scholarship had already reached England.* The two first Headmasters were Wykehamists, John Anwykyll and John Stanbridge, and between them they seem to have devised a new method of teaching grammar, which obtained a wide notoriety : it was prescribed for Manchester Grammar School (1515) and Merchant Taylors' (1560), and the most famous of all the English professors of grammar, William Lily, first High Master of St. Paul's, was among Stanbridge's pupils.

Summing up then the first century of our history we see in the sister-Colleges an acknowledged new model and a nurse of famous schoolmasters. Moreover they gave many able servants to the Crown. Chicheley and Waynflete we have already noticed : Bekington was Privy Seal and Secretary of State : and Andrews, Provost of Eton, and Chandler, Warden successively of

* Adamson, ¦p. 99.

Winchester and New College, also served as Secretary of State. Indeed our tradition seems to have favoured the training of lawyer-administrators of the type of Wykeham himself, rather than philosophers and apologists. Early Wykehamists defended their Church in the senate and in the council-chamber, not in the lecture-room. The

Grocyn

first great name in scholarship is that of William Grocyn, elected to Winchester in 1463, whose medallion looks down from Memorial Buildings : and he brings us out of the Middle Ages to the Renaissance and the Reformation.

There is no reason to doubt that Greek was first taught in Oxford within the walls of New College : and she can thus claim in a sense to be a cradle of the English Renaissance. Some time in the third quarter of the fifteenth century, Warden Chandler invited the Italian scholar, Cornelio Vitelli, to lecture on Greek at New College, and it may well have been from him that Grocyn learnt the rudiments of the language. He afterwards studied in Italy under Politian and Chalchondyles, the foremost scholars of their time, and returning to England in 1491, gave public lectures on Greek at Oxford. Erasmus was among his listeners : and in Grocyn's lecture-room were laid the foundations of his famous friendship with Colet and More. Another Wykehamist of the same company, and their most powerful patron, was William Warham, Archbishop of Canterbury and Chancellor, the last Primate of the old order.

The
Reformation

For the egg which had been laid by Erasmus was now being hatched by Luther : and the progress of the new studies became choked and blocked by the fiercest civil and theological controversies, which at one time threatened to involve in a common ruin all ancient foundations, educational as well as religious. Destruction was happily warded off from the Universities, and from the Colleges of Winchester and Eton by virtue of their intimate connection with the Universities : but from this time forward, until the slumberous calm of the later seventeenth century settled upon the Society, our tradition of *pietas litterata* was ruffled by partisanship and insecurity, no one knowing from day to day where their chance acts or words would lead them. Men of strict principle on both sides suffered deprivation and sometimes exile, while the official opinion of the College, faithfully reflected in the copies of laudatory Latin verses addressed by the scholars to successive sovereigns, veered and shifted from point to point as expediency dictated. No doubt the authorities were wise : there was no room in the Tudor state for anyone but the King, and had his will been crossed, the King would not, for all his boasted friendship to learning, have hesitated to destroy Winchester. As it was, it was an accident that saved us. Further, though Henry was a despot, yet his despotism was of a constitutional order. Constitutional procedure was carefully observed, and it is probably true to say that in attacking the privileges and property of ecclesiastical corporations, the King had the bulk of the nation with him. It was no time for Anselms or Beckets.

Warham died in 1532 *felix opportunitate mortis*. Two years later the papal jurisdiction in England was abolished, Henry being declared by Act of Parliament Supreme Head of the Church of England, and in 1535 commissioners were appointed for the ominous duty of taking a valuation of all property owned by the Church and by ecclesiastical foundations of any sort whatsoever. The College met this first assault with great prudence. Presents were judiciously distributed, a silver salt-cellar to Thomas Cromwell and two oxen, ten sheep, and twelve capons to the King . . . . for his favour in matters concerning the College, and perhaps in consequence of this, Winchester was exempted under an Act of 1536 from the payment to the Crown of the dues hitherto exacted by the See of Rome. In return for this concession Parliament enjoined upon the College the celebration of masses for the King and his family. But greater dangers lay ahead : that same year the dissolution of the monasteries began and with it confiscation on a grand scale. The King had tasted blood and repented him of the former exemptions. In 1539 an Act was passed confirming the suppression of the greater monasteries and in this proscription all Colleges, hospitals and chantries were included. The enactment was repeated in a slightly different form a few years later, empowering the King to take these establishments into possession at his pleasure, and in February 1546 commissions were issued to all parts of the country to ascertain the value of the property to be annexed. Many famous foundations had already disappeared into the pockets of hungry courtiers, and no doubt some filthy bird of prey was waiting for Winchester when by a merciful providence death removed the King in January 1547, and the Act lapsed. A new Chantries Act was passed a few months after, but the Universities, the Colleges of Winchester and Eton, and the Chapel of St. George's, Windsor, were exempted. Winchester and Eton were exempted probably because they were regarded as integral parts of the Universities. Winchester was regarded as a part of Oxford by the University Commissioners of 1857. So the College safely outrode the greatest hurricane of its history. Its neighbours foundered : St. Swithun's was of course suppressed with the other great monasteries and in 1543 Pontissera's College of St. Elizabeth (our neighbour on the eastern side) was granted by the King to Lord Wryothesley. He sold it to Wykeham's College and at one time there was an idea of turning it into an overflow school to provide additional room for Commoners : but our predecessors preferred to demolish it and to use its stones for the extension of Meads Wall. The service of Thurbern's and Fromond's Chantries was suppressed together with the other *obits* under the Act of 1547.

Thereafter the Society took special pains to keep its opinions flexible and to shout as loud for Mary as for Edward and for Elizabeth as for Mary. There were a few recalcitrants ; of the Romanists, the most picturesque figure is John White, the last Catholic Warden and later **Warden** Bishop of Winchester, who dared to preach **White** before Elizabeth from the text " I have praised the dead rather than the living." A number of other Catholic Wykehamists retired to the Low Countries and issued thence a series of books and pamphlets against the Reformation settlement : and another, a Jesuit, Henry Garnet, was executed for complicity in the Gunpowder Plot. On the other side John Philpot was burnt by Bonner in 1555, after a debate in prison with a brother Wykehamist, a Catholic, who failed to move him from his heresies : and there is the celebrated story of William Forde, the Usher, which must **Forde** be set down here in the original :—

" There was many golden images in Wykam's colleage by Wynton. The Churche dore was directly over agaynste the usher's chamber. mr Forde tyed a longe coorde to the images, lynking them all in one coorde, and, being in his chamber after midnight, he plucked the corde's ende, and at one pulle all the golden godes came downe with heyho Rombelo. Yt wakened all men with the rushe. They wer amased at the terryble noyse and also disamayd at the greevous sight . . . . At last they fell to serchyng, but mr Forde, moste suspected, was fownde in his bedd : yet he hadd a dogges lyff among them, Mr Whight the scholemaster, the felows of the howse, and the scholars, crying out and raylyng at him by supportacyone of their master. Lewde men lay in waight for mr Forde many tymes, and one nyght going into the towne he muste neades come whome to the collydge by the towne walles . . . . This was espyed, he was watched, and when he came to a blynd darke corner by Kyngesgate, they layd one hym with staves ; he clapped hys gowne coler, furred with foxe furre, round abowte his head and necke ; they layd on hym some strookes, but by Godes providence the most part, in the great derknes, dyd lyght upon the grownd ; so they ranne away and lefte mr Forde for dede ; but he tumbled and roled hym selfe to the gate, for thei hadd made hym paste goinge : and then he cryed for helpe, and people came to take him up and bare hym to his lodgyng." (Lowth's MS., Camden Society Reprint.)

On the whole, however, partisan passion did not run so high at Winchester as at New College. The scholars were too young to appreciate the significance of the doctrines for which men were burning each other : and the Fellows were not prepared at their time of life to risk the loss of their livelihood. New College, on the other hand, was full of ardent spirits old enough to know and not too old to care, and the tradition of the College being at all times profoundly conservative, some of them strenuously resisted the changes and thereby brought down upon the Society more than one episcopal visitation.

With the decline of the Church's secular influence, our contribution to the public service diminished. Wykehamist Bishops and Deans there were as aforetime ; but Bishops and Deans no longer sat in the Council Chamber. Perhaps it was this consideration that impelled the Society to the wise step of appointing Lord Burghley steward of the manors, a sinecure honour, the bestowal of which amply secured their position at Court. But Winchester's ancient pre-eminence in education remained unimpaired. We gave a model and its first Headmaster to Westminster when it was re-established by Queen Elizabeth in 1560, and when Sir William Harpur endowed Bedford Grammar School in 1566 he named a Wykehamist to preside over it.

One famous political figure appears in our **Sir Henry** sixteenth century portrait gallery, Sir Henry **Wotton** Wotton. He was a Commoner both at Winchester and at New College—a " finger-post " fact in our history as we shall see later. Possessed of a typical Renaissance versatility, he was scholar, physiologist, courtier and diplomatist and bespoke the favour of posterity by having Izaak Walton to write his life. He served as ambassador to the Court of Venice and tradition has fathered upon him the famous saying that a diplomatist is sent " to lie abroad for the benefit of his country." His own invariable practice was to tell the truth : " for you shall never be believed, and by this means your truth will secure yourself if you

173

shall ever be called to an account and it will also put your adversaries, who will still hunt counter, to a loss in all their disquisitions and undertakings." At the end of his life he became Provost of Eton and befriended Milton, who was then living at the neighbouring village of Horton. A letter to him from Wotton was prefixed to the first edition of *Comus*, wherein he speaks of the "Dorique Delicacy in your Songs and Odes, whereunto I must plainly confess to have seen yet nothing parallel in our language."

The Great Rebellion

The Great Rebellion touched us but lightly. There are many stories of destruction averted by faithful Wykehamists holding positions of importance in the Parliamentary Army. They are based on the slenderest evidence : and it is to be feared that our Winchester historians, writing in days when Cromwell had not yet come to his own in posterity's esteem, allowed their royalist fervour to run away with their judgment. So far as our records go there was never any danger either of legalised spoliation or casual looting. In 1642 Parliament exempted the revenues of Winchester, Eton and Westminster from the ordinance sequestering those of Deans and Chapters, and in 1649 it was declared that the Act for the abolition of Deans and Chapters did not extend to Winchester, Eton or Westminster. At New College, as a hundred years before, there were intractable spirits who refused to acknowledge the jurisdiction of the Parliamentary Visitors and were deprived, but at Winchester the current of daily life flowed quietly on, the Society taking all necessary oaths and satisfactory reply being made to the enquiries of the Hampshire Committee of Religion.

The College was not without friends in the Parliamentary party and they possessed in Warden Warden Harris Harris a ruler of rare discretion. It is to be feared he may have sometimes prevaricated in his answers to the Committee ; it was not to be supposed, for example, that the clerks had ever been intended to sing in Chapel or that disaffected practices like organ-playing had ever flourished in the College. But, as Mr. Cook asks, who will judge him ? As his letters show, he abhorred strife ; and at any rate it is not for us, who have profited by his wisdom, to dismiss him as a time-server. He built the front part of Sick House : the rooms at the back were added in 1775 by a Fellow named John Taylor.

School also belongs to this generation. The School number of Commoners had for many years been increasing and extra space was necessary to prevent over-crowding in Seventh. The work was begun in 1683 and finished in 1687, the funds being raised by public subscription. It cannot be asserted in terms that the design is Wren's. The best experts were formerly sceptical : but evidence has lately been adduced showing that the design of the windows is identical with that of the windows in St. Bennet's Church, Upper Thames Street, which was undoubtedly the work of Wren. Wren's builders at St. Bennet's were also employed on School, and we know that Wren was often in Winchester during those years. These facts taken together bring us very close to what we should like to think. Nicholas, the Warden of this period, was a notable builder : he subscribed generously to the cost of School and added largely to the Warden's lodgings. It was apparently in the reign of Harmar (1596-1613) that the Warden, deserting the rooms assigned to him by Wykeham, first began to encroach upon the eastern side of Outer Court.

Four Wykehamists of this epoch deserve to be remembered : Sir Thomas Browne, the physician of Norwich and author of *Religio Medici :* the philosopher Lord Shaftesbury : Thomas Otway, a tragic poet who once stood high in the opinion of good judges, but is now almost forgotten : and Ken Thomas Ken. He returned to Winchester as a Fellow in 1661, and Ken Chamber, which he is supposed to have inhabited, is sacred to his memory. In 1684 he was made Bishop of Bath and Wells and to this day he is accounted among the most famous of the west country Bishops. He was with Monmouth in his last hours, and he and one other Wykehamist—Turner of Ely— were among the seven Bishops whom James II attempted to have convicted for seditious libel. (Lloyd of St. Asaph is usually added : but there is no trace of him in the Winchester records. Some claim him as a Commoner of New College.) The magnitude of the constitutional issue drew all eyes upon them. Ever since 1660 the Church had with a single voice proclaimed the duty of passive obedience to the Crown : and relying upon the support of the clergy and some of the lawyers, James was advancing step by step towards that fixed objective of all his policy—the reduction of England to her former allegiance to Rome. In 1687 he published his first Declaration of Indulgence suspending all penal laws against all classes of Nonconformists, Roman Catholics and Dissenters alike, and dispensing with religious tests. This was an absolutely illegal proceeding and to James' astonishment the first to oppose his will were the clergy, hitherto the foremost champions of Divine Right. The Declaration

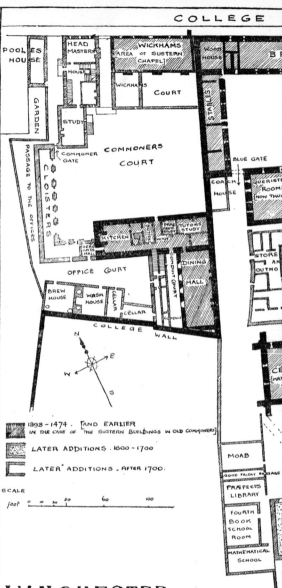

COLLEGE

POOLES HOUSE

HEAD MASTERS HOUSE

WICKHAMS [AREA OF SUSTERN CHAPEL]

WOOD HOUSE

B F

GARDEN

WICKHAMS COURT

STABLES

PASSAGE TO THE OFFICES

STUDY

COMMONER GATE

CLOISTERS

COMMONERS COURT

BLUE GATE

COACH HOUSE

QUERISTE ROOMS [NOW THU]

KITCHEN

PANTRY

HEAD SERVENT STUDY

TUTORS STUDY

DEPT MANS HALL

CONDUIT COURT

DINING HALL

STORE AND OUTHO

OFFICE COURT

BREW HOUSE

WASH HOUSE

CELLAR

CELLAR

CONDUIT

COLLEGE WALL

N
E
W
S

1393-1474. [AND EARLIER
IN THE CASE OF THE SUSTERN BUILDINGS IN OLD COMMONERS]

LATER ADDITIONS. 1600-1700

LATER ADDITIONS. AFTER 1700.

SCALE
feet 0 10 20 30   60   100

CE
MAT

MOAB

GOOD FRIDAY PASSAGE

PRÆFECTS LIBRARY

FOURTH BOOK SCHOOL ROOM

MATHEMATICAL SCHOOL

WINCHESTER COLLEGE
AND
OLD COMMONERS
CIRCA 1835-40

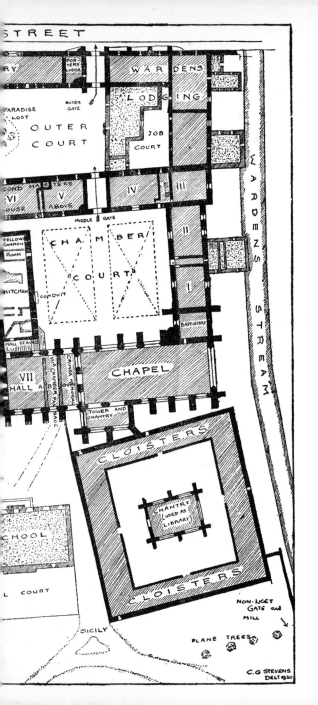

STREET

PORTERS LODGE

PARADISE LOST

OUTER GATE

OUTER COURT

WARDENS LODGING

JOB COURT

VI MASTERS HOUSE

V ABOVE

IV

III

MIDDLE GATE

FELLOWS COMMON ROOM

CHAMBER COURT

KITCHEN

CONDUIT

II

I

BAPTISTRY

HALL STAIRS

VII HALL A

VI CHAMBER PASSAGE

CHAPEL

TOWER AND CHANTRY

WARDENS STREAM

CLOISTERS

CHANTRY (USED AS LIBRARY)

SCHOOL

CLOISTERS

L COURT

SICILY

CLOISTERS

NON-LICET GATE and MILL

PLANE TREES

C. G. STEVENS DELT 1920

was issued again in 1688 and the seven Bishops, with the Primate Sancroft at their head, refused to publish it, addressing to the King at the same time a petition setting forth the reasons for their action. There was a stormy interview with James . . . . ' " This is a standard of rebellion " . . . . " Sir," said Ken, " I hope you will grant us that liberty of conscience which you grant to all mankind . . . . We have two duties to perform, our duty to God and our duty to your Majesty. We honour you : but we fear God . . . . " " Have I deserved this ? " said the King, more and more angry . . . . " I will be obeyed. My Declaration shall be published. You are trumpeters of sedition . . . . I will keep this paper . . . . I will remember that you have signed it . . . . " " God's will be done," said Ken. They were sent to the Tower upon a charge of seditious libel, tried on June 28th—one of the Judges was a Wykehamist —and acquitted amid extraordinary demonstrations of popular favour. But when his principles were at stake, Ken was as indifferent to censure as to applause : for when William of Orange was called to the throne, he refused to abjure his allegiance to James and was deprived of his See. He had published in 1674, while a Fellow, a *Manual of Prayers for the use of the Scholars of Winchester College.*

We are fortunate enough to possess in the Latin hexameter poem *De Collegio Wintoniensi,* by Robert Mathew, scholar of the College, a most valuable picture of our school-life at this period. Mr. A. K. Cook, to whom all Wykehamist antiquaries will acknowledge a debt, has restored the poem to its proper setting as a description of Winchester in the later seventeenth century, not as has been hitherto assumed, in the earlier

Mathew's poem

years of Elizabeth. It is a first-rate source not only for our own history, but for that of English education in general. The Winchester usages of 1647 show a close correspondence with those of Eton as described in Malim's *Consuetudinarium Etonense* of 1560* and as embodied almost wholesale in the Westminster Statutes of that same year. Life in the " three great Seminarys " was strenuous. Our predecessors rose at 5, work started at 6, and three intolerable hours of study followed before any food was taken : from about 10 to 12 more work, then dinner and work again afterwards till 5, with an interval in summer for " bevers " : supper at 5 and bed soon after 8. On Tuesdays and Thursdays there were remedies and most of the day was spent on Hills. The authors read were : among the Greeks, Homer, Musaeus, Hesiod and Theognis : of the Romans, Virgil, some of Cicero's philosophical works, Horace, Ovid and Terence : and the most famous school-book of that age, Erasmus's *Colloquies*, a collection of Latin conversations intended to impart a purity of style and at the same time to arm the youth for the formal disputations which since the days of Quintilian had filled so great a place in higher education. By the seventeenth century the use of Latin in ordinary conversation was beginning to die out, " but in 1639 eighteen scholars bound themselves to speak no other language in school, hall, chambers and every place where they assembled, on pain of being esteemed guilty of sin towards God and infamy among men." The curriculum faithfully reflects that conservative and clerical tradition which ruled in the Universities, rendering them quite unsuitable for the

Daily Life

* Cook, Appendix VII, p. 549.

training of any except professional scholars and candidates for Orders, and it is worth remarking that Bacon and Milton in their plans for the spread of learning assign no function to the Universities. Greek had appeared some time early in the sixteenth century—precisely when we cannot be certain——and in Mathew's time it was confined to the upper part of the School. It is satisfactory to learn from another source that at Winchester "they use no word-books nor *janua linguarum* but high classick authors " : plain texts, no commentaries or other *impedimenta*. Lord Selborne (1825—1830) speaks of one boy taking up the whole *Iliad*. Set declamations were common : and we have a hint about " Standing-up," an art which in later years was carried to a high degree of perfection, enormous masses of the classical writings being committed to memory. There was no modern language teaching earlier than 1821 and before 1834 there was no regular mathematical master. Such mathematics as could be had were dispensed by the writing-master, whose occupation, according to T. A. Trollope (1820—1828), seemed confined principally to mending pens and adding up marks. But in her own field of classical learning Winchester excelled. So long was the list of Wykehamist prizemen at the University in the later years of the eighteenth century that a writer in the *Gentleman's Magazine* made public complaint that Minerva must have been imprisoned within the walls of the College, so great a share of her inspiration had she vouchsafed us. In the darkest days this standard was maintained.

To those dark days we have now come : and **Abuses** when we look for the causes of the decline, we find that they had been silently at work ever since

the Reformation. The Reformation was the end
of the old Collegiate life. Signs of its break-up
may be observed at the end of the sixteenth
century and a hundred years later the process was
complete. The first sign was the desertion by
Warden Bilson (1580—1596) of the common table
in Hall. He was the first married Warden and
Mrs. Bilson was the first woman to live in the
College. The ten Priest-Fellows whom Wykeham
installed to conduct the elaborate ritual of the old
faith were now without an occupation. They
gradually ceased to keep residence, preferring to
retire to their country livings, but continuing to
draw their emoluments and sometimes—it would
be hard to credit this, had not specific mention
been made of it in episcopal injunctions—selling
to the College the wheat that was too poor to
find a market in their own villages. The obligations of their trust were disregarded : the College
and its endowments existed, it was believed, for
the comfort of the Society—that is the Warden
and Fellows : the children were an adjunct, which
had, it is true, to be provided for, but possessing
no claim to a share in the rapidly increasing
revenues. The men employed to teach them were
so seriously underpaid as to be compelled to accept
gratuities from their pupils in defiance of the
Statutes : the scholars were kept out of Meads in
order that the Fellows, mostly absentees, might
enjoy the pleasures of contemplation there without
danger of disturbance : and for such improvements as were made in their food and general
comfort they were indebted to private benefactors.
As late as 1860, while the Warden received £1750
and the ten Fellows £6598 a year between them,
not more than £1035 was set apart for the payment
of teachers. That was six years before Dr.

Ridding's appointment. In 1834 the sum so appropriated was £250.

The sister-College at Oxford had already begun to drift into the same backwater. As its distinguished historians have shown, the Great Rebellion left a permanent mark upon Oxford : it was never again a place of study as it had been in the Middle Ages, and the effects of this change made themselves felt with special malignity in a close corporation like New College. There are a great number of references in contemporary papers to drinking, gaming, coffee-house loafing and other disorders in the College : and the infection quickly spread to Winchester. The philosopher Lord Shaftesbury wrote in 1689 of Winchester that there were scarcely any " that escape ye Mother vice of drinking," and of New College " That Palmer was ye only sober man of it." The inconveniences of an unalterable code now became manifest : the arrangements so carefully planned by the Founder for the encouragement of diligence merely served in this new atmosphere to foster idleness. Now that study had gone out of fashion, there was no incentive to effort : once a Winchester scholar had secured his election to New College his future was assured. He passed in due course to a Fellowship, obtained his degree as a matter of right, and either lived on at Oxford in comfort all his life or dozed away his days in a College living. He might also return to the equal repose of a Winchester Fellowship. It was a matter of general comment in the University how few were the numbers of our eminent *alumni* at that time : Archbishop Laud had asked the Bishop of Winchester as early as 1635 whether means could not be found of removing this reproach, and

Antony Wood quotes a saying that New College men were golden scholars, silver bachelors, leaden masters and wooden doctors. Of the distinguished Wykehamists from Sir Henry Wotton to Bishop Ridding the great majority failed of their election *ad Oxon*, thus escaping the prevalent paralysis.

At Winchester places upon the foundation were to all intents and purposes for sale, though when George I tried to establish his right to nominate, Wardens Bigg and Dobson withstood him. Fellowships were largely confined to a small circle of Wykehamical families : and late in the seventeenth century the noxious practice arose of electing the Warden of New College to succeed to the Wardenship of Winchester—a state of affairs never contemplated by the Founder. This happened seven times between 1679 and 1757 and might have continued for another century had not the Bishop of Winchester disallowed the election of Purnell in the latter year. There could only be one reason why the Warden of New College, the acknowledged head of the whole Foundation, should have hankered for the inferior place. New College may have been the higher rack but Winchester was the deeper manger . . . . " It was easier for the Warden of Winchester to increase his emoluments at the expense of his helpless charity-boys and a very small number of Fellows, than for the Head of the great and highly-organised corporation at Oxford to monopolise the increasing value of the College estates." In 1708 the Fellows revolted against the encroachments of the Warden and a disgraceful quarrel broke out between them, ending in a suit in Chancery. The children were left to fare as they might on meagre commons. Sometimes the Bishop of Winchester intervened on their behalf, and sometimes, as in the incident of 1708 quoted above, when thieves fell out, honest men came by their own : for the Fellows, to annoy the Warden, increased the allowances of meat and beer in Hall.

The security against abuses provided by the Founder, the annual scrutiny held at Election-time, dwindled to a form : and as the eighteenth century wore on, the neglect of the authorities bore fruit in rebellion and general unhappiness. Winchester was not alone : the same tendencies showed themselves everywhere in a disregard of founders' intentions, a pedantic adherence to custom, and an indifference to the welfare of the scholars so great as almost to amount to a historical curiosity. Locke had noticed some years before the rough life, the harsh discipline and lax stand-ards of conduct in the great schools : and the reports of the Public School and the Schools Enquiry Commissioners told the same story many times over. Sydney Smith, speaking of his days at Winchester (1782—1788) described the whole system as " one of abuse, neglect and vice " : and unfortunately there is no reason to question the substantial accuracy of his account.

One voice was raised in protest against the prevailing practices. Mr. Cook has told us how Warden Bigg (1729—1740) tried in the last months **Warden** of his life to persuade the Fellows that they had **Bigg** obligations towards the scholars, who were as much members of the Foundation as themselves : how he appealed to them to help him in correct-ing abuses : and how they waved him away. He was a hundred years too soon.

In 1724 Dr. Burton was appointed Headmaster. **Burton** He is remembered as the founder of Old Com- **and Old** moners. Commoners were of course no novelty : **Commoners**

ten were admitted under Statute to residence in
the College, and they were joined in very early
times by day-boys from the town, who in 1412
numbered from eighty to a hundred. In later
years the number of those living in the College
exceeded the accommodation available in the
rooms of the Headmaster and the Usher, and
for some years at the beginning of the seventeenth
century the Headmaster is found in occupation
of rooms in the Sustern Spital : it is very probable
that he took boarders there. Dr. Burton came
into possession of those quarters in 1738, and
started at once upon the alterations and additions
to the Spital premises necessary to erect the new
boarding house. His buildings—Old Commoners
—were ready for use in 1742, the Usher being
placed in charge. The portraits hanging in the
Second Master's dining room give us a good idea
of " Dr. Burton's gentlemen "—men of the world,
all of them, with a practised Parliamentary
manner, acquired apparently in their cradles.
The number of Commoners fluctuated considerably throughout the century, affording us a fair
barometric chart of the School's progress. In
1702 there were 49 : then a suspicion of Jacobitism
hung about the College and the numbers fell.
In 1716 the Grand Jury of Hampshire presented
us for " disaffection and corruption of manners " :
and in 1718 the Secretary of State complained
officially to the Warden that on the anniversary
of George I's accession many of the scholars
came into Cathedral with crape hat-bands. In
Dr. Burton's early years the numbers mounted
to 123, but had fallen again to 39 in 1765, and so
on, backwards and forwards until the Headmastership of Dr. Goddard, a period of unbroken
prosperity. Commoners were at no time popular

with the Warden and Fellows : considering the
scholars as an adjunct to themselves, Commoners
they looked upon as an adjunct to an adjunct.
No intercourse was permitted between them and
the scholars, except when they met in School.

Burton was succeeded by the Usher, Dr. Joseph Joseph
Warton. A discriminating critic, a poet, a wit, Warton
a friend of Dr. Johnson and a member of his
famous circle, one wonders how he ever took to
schoolmastering. Boys with tastes akin to his
own found him an inspiring teacher : but literary
life in London would have suited him much
better. He was once brave enough to stand up
to the despot of Fleet Street :—

> *Johnson :* Sir, I am not used to be contradicted.

> *Warton :* Better for yourself and friends, Sir,
> if you were. Our admiration for you could
> not be increased, but our love might—

but he was not brave enough to face an unruly
class or to quell an incipient riot. His reign was
a period of chronic disorder. Rebellions broke The
out in 1770, 1774, 1778 and 1793 ; the last was Rebellions
the most serious and ended in Dr. Warton's
retirement. A College Prefect had gone in
defiance of the Warden's order to listen to the
band of the Bucks Militia playing in the Close,
and Warden Huntingford, hearing of it, stopped
the whole School their Easter leave-out. It
was the year of the execution of Louis XVI
and examples of resistance to tyranny were not
wanting. The forty seniors bound themselves by
oath to stand together : the keys were taken
from the porter and the Warden barricaded in
his own house, together with the Second Master,
Goddard. Huntingford applied for help to the
High Sheriff, but that officer, observing that the

paving stones of Chamber Court had been carried to the top of Outer Gate and the parapet loosened for discharge upon the enemy, withdrew for the time. Peace was finally restored through the Sheriff's mediation, but an act of ill-faith on the part of Huntingford tempted the boys to the rash step of resigning their places in the College. To their surprise the Warden accepted the resignations with the utmost satisfaction and thirty-five left.

It was not Winchester alone whose peace was thus troubled. Rebellion broke out six times at Eton between 1728 and 1832 : and similar disorders occurred at Harrow in 1771 and 1818, and at Rugby in 1797 and 1822.

Goddard The gloomy monotony of Huntingford's long reign was lightened in 1793 by the appointment of William Stanley Goddard to the Headmastership. His title to our affectionate remembrance is two-fold. First, he was Arnold's master : and it is not rash to conjecture that of the many noble traditions that Arnold gave to English education, the most life-giving of all was derived from the example of Goddard. . . . . " The honourable compact," wrote a contemporary, " between Dr. Goddard and the boys worked a reformation in the School, the object of everyone's observation and praise. Manly reason and liberal confidence were reciprocally made the current medium of his management : and the effect of it was that every boy became a gentleman and a boy of honour." This description might be applied line by line to Arnold's own work : and if we can believe that Arnold did in any measure catch his inspiration from Goddard, then is Goddard great indeed. Secondly, he gave a large sum of money to increase the salaries of the masters, putting an end thereby to the degrading and unstatuteable practice of receiving gratuities, to which we have already referred.

The hands of the clock were set back for a time when Gabell was appointed in 1809 to succeed Goddard. He was an able teacher but without Goddard's genius for a liberal discipline : and the fifth and last of the rebellions broke out in 1818. A Commoner Tutor had been guilty of a breach of confidence : he had invited some Prefects to dinner and in the course of the evening had learnt from them that they sometimes went " up town " without leave asked. Huntingford was informed and certain restrictions were introduced. The School declared war forthwith, the Warden was again imprisoned and the College placed in a state of siege. The Warden, who was also Bishop of Hereford, made himself ridiculous by threatening to bring the ringleaders on their knees before the House of Lords for imprisoning a peer of Parliament ; and finally took refuge in a breach of faith worse than that of 1793. The boys were promised a fortnight's holiday if they would surrender : they immediately accepted the terms, but on their way to the town were met in a narrow place by a company of soldiers and chivied back to the College. Twenty were expelled, among them W. P. Wood, afterwards Lord Chancellor Hatherley. It is satisfactory to learn that Huntingford's action was " emphatically condemned " at the next scrutiny, the Commoner Tutor being removed.

In 1832 Warden Huntingford died. He had administered the estates with prudence, but—to say the least of it—he was singularly ill-suited by temperament to preside over a great School. With him the old order passed away : for though his successor, Barter, was in theory as much opposed to innovation as himself, yet Barter was a man of broad humanity and very early in his reign improvements were introduced for the greater comfort of the boys, and the ancient barrier between College and Commoners was broken down. A spirit of change was abroad : the Reform Act of 1832 was followed by a process of adjustment and renovation which made itself felt in every department of national life. Education was no exception. Sixteen years earlier, in 1816, a Committee of the House of Commons had been set up under the chairmanship of Henry Brougham to enquire into " the education of the lower orders," and the terms of reference were stretched to include the ancient endowed schools. Whatever we may think of Brougham, he had at least the insight to perceive that the revolution in industrial methods and the consequent increase in the population was making the education of the people a question of urgent national importance : and the first objective in his campaign was to purify the administration of educational charities and to ensure that, so far as possible, they should be made to serve the purposes for which they were intended.

A word about the celebrities of the eighteenth and early nineteenth centuries before we pass to the new age. Winchester bred minor poets in great profusion—most of them so very minor that they cannot claim a place in any but the most ample history of English literature. William Collins, admitted in 1733, left a greater name. He lived a miserable life and lost his reason before he died : but the Odes *To Evening* and *To the Passions* are among the masterpieces of our language. Other shorter pieces, too, there are, of a rare beauty, which deserve to be better known. Among Churchmen, William Howley became Archbishop of Canterbury. There were some famous fighting men—in the Navy, Admiral Keats, of the *Superb*, of whom Nelson said that his person alone was equal to one French '74 ; several Peninsular generals, the best known, perhaps, Sir John Colborne, Lord Seaton, who broke the final charge of the Old Guard at Waterloo ; many politicians, Speaker Onslow, Speaker Addington (afterwards Prime Minister but a poor creature), Lord Cardwell, the Army reformer, and Robert Lowe ; and three Lord Chancellors, Lords Cranworth, Hatherley and Selborne.

Warden Barter and Dr. Moberly held office **Moberly** together for nearly thirty years, and they worked throughout in the closest sympathy with each other. Neither of them were great reformers, but they accomplished much valuable work. A gradual change came over the *ethos* of the School ; ancient barbarisms died out, our tradition responded to the movements then quickening in Church and State and its old vitality began to return. Of the visible memorials that Barter and Moberly left behind them, the most important was New Commoners, which was begun **New** in 1839. The venture was not a success : the **Commoners** subsoil was unhealthy, epidemics of fever recurred continually and in 1856 the numbers sank to 68. That was the low-water mark ; and ten years later when Dr. Moberly retired not only was Commoners full, but three boarding-houses had been opened outside the precincts to accommodate the overflow.

In 1866 the Warden and Fellows, knowing not what they were doing, appointed George

Ridding to succeed Dr. Moberly : and within
the eighteen odd years of his Headmastership,
the revolution, or rather the restoration, was
practically complete. The time was favourable.
The Universities and the greater Public Schools
were in the travail of a new birth : they and
their works had been subjected to a close investigation by Royal Commissions between 1854 and
1864, and in accordance with precedent, the
University Commissioners had treated Winchester
as an integral part of Oxford. The Founder's
Statutes were partly superseded at both Colleges
in 1857 by Ordinances drawn up by the Commissioners : the privileges of Founder's kin were
abolished, and scholarships and Fellowships at
New College were within certain limits thrown
open to non-Wykehamists. Further changes were
introduced under the Public Schools Act, 1868,
which followed the Report of the Commissioners.
The Warden and Fellows were given a period of
grace in which to reform themselves : but they
resisted to the last and in 1871 their powers were
transferred to the new Governing Body. The
new Statutes, drawn up by them and approved
by Her Majesty in Council, came into operation
in 1874.

In those years of indecision Ridding saw his
chance to strike and he struck hard. Between
1867 and 1871 six new Houses were started,
Commoners was abolished and classrooms set
up upon the site, Moberly Library was opened,
the original bathing-place in Dalmatia and a
boat-house were provided, the land beyond
Meads Wall, once called New Field and now
properly re-christened Riddings Field, purchased
and turned into a cricket ground, and Lavender
Meads converted from a swampy uneven expanse

into the beautiful level we know. The contribution of the Foundation towards the cost of these changes was confined to the purchase of that part of the property owned by the Dean and Chapter, and to the sacrifice of the revenue from that part which belonged to the College : nor was a penny raised by public subscription. The rest came out of the private resources of the Headmaster and not more than half of the £20,000 he spent was refunded to him.

Of that more enduring memorial of his greatness, his influence upon his pupils, it were superfluous to say anything : for fortunately there are some who can speak of it at first hand. At first some of his contemporaries dreaded his reforming zeal. They need not have trembled : for it was not as if a stranger had been let loose upon us, or an ignorant *doctrinaire*. There was no greater master of Wykehamical tradition and Wykehamical lore. " . . . . Born in these walls," as he said of himself, " it has only been for short intervals that I have not had my home in them," and his wife has told us how wisely he guided the deliberations of his new and untried Governing Body and how much we owe to him for what he retained as well as for what he altered. In 1872 College itself, as an institution, came within a hair's breadth of abolition ; Dr. Ridding secured its preservation. One of those who feared most from his early policy came in the end to acknowledge his services in the most generous terms any Wykehamist could frame. " . . . . I said Ridding was going to ruin the School," remarked the late Warden of New College in 1887 : " now I say he is our Second Founder." Not the least of his works was the establishment in 1880 of the School Mission at All Hallows, East India Dock. The

Mission was transferred in 1882 to Landport, and in 1908 to Rudmore, where St. John the Baptist's Church was built and consecrated in 1916.

In 1884 Dr. Fearon returned from Durham to Winchester to carry on the work of his friend and leader George Ridding ; and no one was better qualified to do so. He resigned in 1901, but to the end of his life he worked and lived for Winchester, and it was his pride that he had attended more than seventy Domums. The two men were animated by the same liberal spirit, but this was to be seen in the development of teaching and of the staff rather than in bricks and mortar, for which little money was available in the last years of the 19th century. It is true a School Sanatorium was needed, and in 1886 one was built ; and Wykehamists have grown as accustomed to the sight of its pepper-boxes in Meads as they have to the presence of seagulls : but it still looks like an alien which has strayed here from the Bournemouth cliffs. The west side of Meads saw another addition ten years later when Old Wykehamists helped by their subscriptions to celebrate the 500th anniversary of the Foundation, and Basil Champneys was asked to build the Museum, officially known as " Memorial Buildings." The colonnade facing Meads has beauty, but the upper facades are over-rich in ornament and the building is crowned by an ugly roof : still it has proved of great value to many generations, with its twin gallery divided between art (classical and mediaeval) and natural science. Dr. Fearon himself presented the interesting collection of Hampshire birds. In his latter years came the South African War, and he planned the erection of a new Commoner Gate in Kingsgate

Street as a memorial to Wykehamists who lost their lives in it—a memorial through which all future generations were to pass in their daily life. The foundation stone of this gate, designed by an Old Wykehamist, F. L. Pearson, was laid by Lord Roberts in 1902.

Dr. Burge came in 1901 when the Warden and **Burge** Fellows were able to sanction fresh building schemes ; and under his rule the School became better equipped to deal with the sciences of which the last century scarcely realized the full importance. Music School, in Roman's Road, was opened in 1904 to the design of Edward Prior : it is seemly and beautiful within, if somewhat clumsy in the outline of its roof. In the same year Mr. Henry Hill reared Science School in Lavender Meads, with a facade perhaps too ornate for its purpose : subsequent additions by Mr. T. D. Atkinson show a more modern spirit and a severer taste. In 1909 Mr. F. L. Pearson was again called in to continue his work by Commoner Gate. He designed an Armoury for the O.T.C., and a group of fives courts, whose plain flint wall harmonizes well with the wayward charm of Kingsgate Street. In the haphazard grouping of stone, flint and brick buildings which lie west of Meads this is the happiest addition.

But the finest bit of original work there is the new Cloister. Dr. Rendall, who had succeeded to **Rendall** the Headmastership in 1911, inspired by memories of the Great War and working in the happiest collaboration with Sir Herbert Baker, the architect of Pretoria and Imperial Delhi, has left us a worthy memorial of those tragic days and their heroic sacrifice. Their achievement—cloistered court, columns of Hopton stone, Cotswold roofing, carved tablets, woodwork and iron work, with the words of Dr. Rendall's own composition binding the whole together—these have won the affection of Wykehamists and the praises of many visitors. Apart from this, Dr. Rendall's artistic judgement found scope in restoring and adapting those parts of College where opportunities had been missed in previous work. His hand may be seen in the re-shaping of Moberly Court, in the restoration of School (where Mr. Atkinson had a good field for his taste and his knowledge of the arts), in the fitting up of the Drawing School above Chantry, and above all in the furnishing of Chapel, where Mr. W. D. Caroe was commissioned to clothe the nakedness which Butterfield had left. Wykeham's Chapel had lost so much in the 19th century ; its successor has striven to repair the loss and to give dignity and beauty once more to the house of God.

Dr. Rendall resigned in 1924 soon after the formal opening of the War Cloister by the Duke of Connaught : and after such a period of activity the next ten years were bound to be quieter. But if our rulers have been compelled to mark time and to wait for better years before they crown Sir Herbert Baker's scheme with the Hall, which he designed to open out from the N.W. corner of his Cloister, much has been done unofficially.

Williams Dr. Williams has found out or stimulated private donors who have wished to commemorate their connection with the School as pupils or parents. To them we owe the two cricket pavilions associated with the names of J. E. Frazer and the sons of Mr. R. L. Hunter—the new Ridding Gate and inscription presented by North Country Wykehamists—the new gate into Moberly Court, presented by Wykehamist members of the two Houses of Parliament, bearing the portcullis of

St. Stephen's, Westminster—and the bridge over Logie at the south end of the Warden's garden, the gift of an anonymous Wykehamist. In most of these changes Professor R. M. Y. Gleadowe has been the chief adviser, often the designer ; and it is to him that College owes the new glass in Hall. Designed by a Wykehamist, cut, leaded and painted in College, by those who work in and for the School, it is as surely a product of Winchester as the illuminated manuscripts of mediaeval days ; and it has enriched and beautified one of our most precious buildings. It is chiefly of " pattern " kind into which are worked heraldic shields with the arms of a select number of famous Old Wykehamists.

One big scheme which Dr. Williams has initiated, the conversion of the old Brewery in Outer Court into a School Library, is not yet finished while this book is in the press.* The growth of the Library has hardly kept pace in this century with the development of science, music and art : books and readers will now have more space in more attractive surroundings, and a part of College which had become obsolete will wake to a new lease of life. We can imagine the delight of the Founder, who as a true son of the Middle Ages was always ready to adapt and re-build, and who would not have wished to keep a 14th century brewhouse as a museum specimen, when his " children " were in need of space. Under the direction of Sir Herbert Baker new

* This book, written by members of the School and primarily for them, naturally dates its events by the reigns of succeeding Headmasters as English history is divided by the reigns of its sovereigns; but all Wykehamists should be aware what the School owes to the wisdom and the labours of Wardens and Fellows, who control all building schemes and give them the most careful consideration.

windows have been opened, chiefly southwards to Outer Court : the eastern half is to be a lofty reading-room rising from the ground to the rafters : the western half will be divided into two floors for the storage of books. Within the narrow limits prescribed by Kingsgate Street and the river the College is now making full use of its inheritance.

An Appendix to the Outlines of English Mediaeval Architecture

IT is difficult to classify any art. To classify chronologically according to date is most difficult of all. But English mediaeval architecture does really fall into a series of periods during each of which a certain style is used to the exclusion of all others. There are of course transitional periods and differences between the dates at which a style is generally adopted or generally superseded in the great towns on the one hand and in the country on the other. But the main thesis remains true : at a certain date in England, say 1220, the whole country was in a certain manner ; at a later date, say 1320, the earlier manner had lost favour and all buildings were designed in a new but no less uniform style. In mediaeval architecture, indeed, there is no fixed *tradition* of building, but only a clear and ever-moving *evolution*, or development. This development will now be summarised under a series of headings, these being the names given, somewhat arbitrarily, to the chief styles in England between 700 and 1500.

ANGLO-SAXON.

The period that is before the Norman Conquest. **Before 1066** Its chief characteristic is that it shows by very clear traces that it is an *imitation of timber construction*. Often these are stone bars, as it were beams, built in with a wall of flints to strengthen them. The pillars are short and squat, resembling balusters, as if they had been turned with a lathe : and they are often topped by plain square blocks for capitals. At the corners of the building is found the very characteristic *Long and Short* work : that is, long stones are placed alternately in a vertical and horizontal position. The windows and arches have round (or sometimes triangular) heads. The stone work is coarse, and worked entirely with the axe. The best example near Winchester is the Church at HEADBOURNE WORTHY ; the stone " beams " and long-and-short work being clearly marked. At Corhampton in the Meon Valley a little Saxon nave and chancel arch remain almost untouched. The pilaster-strips on the walls are very characteristic.

See diagram
p. 199

1050—1200. NORMAN.

Even before the Conquest architects from Normandy had arrived in England along with the foreign favourites of Edward the Confessor. But in the first thirty years after the Conquest there was a regular furore for building cathedrals : and nearly all our greatest Churches were now first reared in the NORMAN style. Its keynote is *massiveness ;* there are very few signs that the architects understood construction. To make a building stand they made its walls immensely thick, with small narrow windows deeply set within them. These walls were not solid stone-work as they appear to be inside and out, but are filled with rubble. Norman walls therefore often bulged, cracked and even fell. Columns are low and massive, sometimes polygonal, sometimes circular. Their windows and arches are easily recognised, for they have *semi-circular heads.*

The Evolution of the Window & Tracery.

N. B. These figures are not drawn to scale.

S = Saxon.
N = Norman.
E.E. = Early English, &c.
G = Geometrical.
C = Curvilinear.
R = Reticulated.
F = Flamboyant.
P = Perpendicular.
Tr = Transitional.

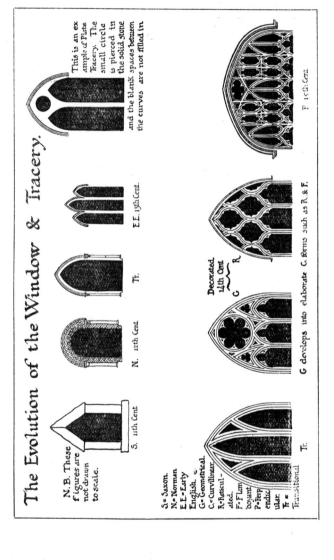

S. 11th Cent.

N. 12th Cent.

Tr.

E.E. 13th Cent.

This is an example of Plate Tracery. The small circle is pierced in the solid stone and the blank spaces between the curves are not filled in

Tr.

Decorated. 14th Cent.
G ⁓ R

G develops into elaborate C. forms such as R. & F.

F. 15th Cent.

They seldom made vaulted roofs of stone,* but preferred timber roofs. The latter place no special strain or outward thrust upon the walls as an arched vault does : therefore the Normans had less need to support the wall externally by buttresses. The Norman buttress is no more than a thickening of the strong ashlar skin of the wall at those places where the main outward thrusts from beams or vaults occur. The masonry is rude, originally cemented by very broad layers of mortar, but later in the period the mortar spaces became narrower. The ornament is also primitive, for the masons still only used the axe. With this clumsy instrument they decorated their windows and doorways, using the ornamentation known as Zig-zag most frequently of all.

The Transepts of Cathedral exhibit nearly all the characteristics above mentioned, and the tower (rebuilt 30 years or more later) shows the narrower mortaring as well as the use of Zig-zag ornament.

* In the aisles of the transepts in the Cathedral is Norman vaulting, as also at St. Cross. In the latter case, however, the exception proves the rule, for the arches of the Norman vaulting have become pointed, and we are in fact no longer in the Norman period proper but on the threshold of Early English. In fact, it was precisely the *introduction of the stone vaulting that necessitated the introduction of the pointed arch.* The problem that met the builders was this :—It is required to give to a rectangular space A B C D a roof vaulted more or less like a dome. To do this, we must first span with arches the spaces, AB, BC, CD, DA, before filling in the vault. This is easy, if all the four spaces are of an equal span, for then the arches will all be of an equal height. But suppose that our rectangle is not a square, and suppose therefore that AB and CD are twice the span of BC and DA, then the arches spanning BC and DA will fall miserably short of the other two, and so of the proper level of the vault. The only neat way to bring them up to that height is by *carrying them to a point.*

In the second half of the twelfth century a change was slowly coming. At St. Cross or Romsey* it is very marked. The work becomes less coarse. The stone vault begins to appear, and though the pointed head is used at St. Cross for those arches which have to bear weight, the windows and other purely decorative arches still remain round-headed.

The builders are beginning to learn the principles of construction, and how to counteract the tendency of an arched stone roof to thrust the walls outwards. Their solution was the buttress. The south wall of the Nave of St. Cross is well worth studying from outside—there are three windows, the one to the east pure Norman, round and unadorned ; the one to the west is pointed and typically Early Gothic. Now observe the buttresses ; the one answering to the Norman window is flat and shallow, hardly protruding from the wall, designed to carry but little extra weight. The Early English buttress projects in steps or sets-off, and is designed to resist pressure coming on the wall from within the Church. That is the principle upon which every true Gothic building is framed and compacted. It is an intricate and nicely calculated skeleton of stone, in which the arches within strive, like " bended bows," to burst outwards, while the external buttressings and props meet and restrain this pressure.

1200—1300. Early English.

True Gothic begins in England with what is called the Early English period : and it follows that what we must look for in the churches of

* In each case the earlier work is to the east, and the style develops as you move westwards.

this date is a better sense of construction ; the walls need no longer be many feet thick ; the fabric rests on the buttresses, and will not be weakened if pierced by more frequent windows— the interior will be capped by lofty vaults. The note of the whole building will be *lightness*.

The windows are *pointed*, often mere *lancets* ; glass (of which there was next to none in Norman buildings) will now claim more and more space : gradually the windows will grow larger, and *tracery* will soon be needed to help carry the glass by the support of its mullions. Then again, just when this attempt to lighten buildings began, the chisel came into use, and things became possible which the axe could not perform. The pillars hitherto so solidly massed become detached, and often stand out, as they do at SALISBURY, in a cluster round the central shaft, but separate from it. The chisel, too, can carve the capitals in the likeness of foliage, which is at first conventional when more is thought of the pattern and general form than of the exact imitation of real leaves. *Dog-tooth* mouldings are the favourite decoration round doorways in place of the old Zig-zag. The dog-tooth pattern is really only four tongues or leaves meeting at an apex. The mason revelled in the use of his new tool, and carried even to excess the under-cutting and hollowing out of his capitals and mouldings. We need go no further than DE LUCY's work in CATHEDRAL to see how odd a contrast is the lightness of this style to the work of Norman builders of a century before.

With the next century we come to the
DECORATED style. The process of adornment
has been continued : and it is marked, as its
name suggests, by an extreme *richness* of ornament.
The space available for stained glass is increasing ;
the desire for light in our dark northern land is
becoming more and more obvious. Windows are
larger ; the clerestory (namely, the windows seen
high up above the aisles) is growing larger also ;
the triforium, or gallery, below the clerestory, is
diminishing in proportion. With this increase of
window space comes greater ingenuity in devising
window-tracery.

At first the patterns in the window heads were
strictly *Geometric* : circles, trefoils, triangles, and
so forth. Very magnificent examples of these
may be seen in ST. JOHN'S CHURCH and in the
west front of ST. CROSS, and east end of ROMSEY.
Here the designer has thought only of the shape
of aperture, punched as it were through a sheet
of stone. The window from inside has the
beauty of stars shining out of darkness. Little
by little, however, they came to design their
windows on a different principle, as if they were
dealing no longer with a pattern of light on dark,
but with lines of dark on light ; they take the
mullions or vertical stone bars of the window
as the basis of their design, and obtain a pattern
by interlacing these in the window head. This
style is sometimes called *curvilinear*. Though
Ruskin thought it decadent, it produced some
of the most magnificent windows. In the NORTH
TRANSEPT of CATHEDRAL there are some fine
examples inserted in the Norman work.

Finally, the ornamentation throughout is
becoming more and more elaborate and profuse.

The capitals are, as a rule, less deeply undercut than in the preceding century ; the foliage is more an imitation of real leaves and the natural growth of oak, maple, ivy, and vine. The " ball-flower " ornament is lavishly dotted round doors and windows. A profusion of grotesque carved heads appear in gargoyles or on the ends of dripstones (the projecting ledges over windows). Every gable-end or buttress has its finial or decorative top - knot. Within, the aisles are crowded with highly ornamented tombs, shrines, and wooden screens, and the choirs filled with carved wooden stalls such as those in CATHEDRAL. So the workers of the fourteenth century wrought every elaboration of their fancy in the adornment of the insides and outsides of their churches, and then architecture undergoes a sudden sobering.

1380—1500. PERPENDICULAR.

From about the middle of the century we can trace a change. Whether their vitality was sapped by the Black Death of 1350, or whether they suddenly realised that they, and still more the French with their Flamboyant windows and flame tracery, were trying to twist and twine stone bars about in a fashion more suited to basket-work or wrought iron, in any case the English architects suddenly changed their tactics, and between the years 1380 and 1400 discarded the Decorated, adopting in its place a style invented about 1340 at Gloucester for the purpose of transforming the appearance of a Norman choir without removing any of the masonry. The chief characteristics of this new style are equally apparent in the choir at Gloucester, remodelled in 1344, and in the nave at Winchester, rebuilt and remodelled from 1350 to 1410 by

EVOLUTION OF GOTHIC DETAIL

VAULTING

ROMANESQUE

GOTHIC

French

English

CAPITALS

Winchester
NORMAN

Bridlington
EARLY ENGLISH

Southwell
DECORATED

Piddleton
PERPENDICULAR

ORNAMENT

NORMAN

EARLY ENGLISH

DECORATED

PERPENDICULAR

BUTTRESSES

1 NORMAN 1160

2 EARLY ENGLISH 1220

3 DECORATED 1360

4 PERPEND^R 1470

1   2   3   4

Edyngton and Wykeham. The windows are divided up into rows of rectangular compartments, the head of the window alone being elaborate in design. Wall spaces are also panelled in this way. The name Perpendicular which is given to this style is not a good one. Horizontal would be better. All Gothic is perpendicular in its especial tendency to use upward moving lines, late English Gothic alone introduced a free use of horizontals in transoms and cornices and in the square-headed frames of doors and windows. The desire to make churches very light leads to the practical extinction of the triforium. This was the age of great areas of stained glass ; the framework of the structure becomes more and more of a skeleton. Great use is made of *flying buttresses*, which give a graceful effect to the exterior with their pinnacled endings. The columns are less massive (Winchester Cathedral is not typical in this, since Wykeham was re-moulding a massive Norman Nave, not building afresh). Capitals are less effectively moulded, and foliage becomes more feeble and more conventional again. The typical ornaments are the *fleur-de-lys*, Tudor rose, and portcullis, both in wood and stonework. The glass was perhaps too much given up to pictorial effects, and the general effect is rather one of confusion than of beauty. As we approach Tudor times, the vaultings, already marvels of dexterity, become more and more fantastic, and are often provided with pendants hanging like stalactites from the ceiling. The window arch tends to be depressed until it is almost *flat or square-headed*, and so we arrive upon the threshold of the Renaissance.

The course of development is a natural one throughout. The heavy Norman buildings with small windows, admitting only a very dim religious light, were not really suited to gloomy England. In southern or eastern lands where to enter a dim lit church from the brilliance of the noonday sun is both restful and impressive, the small windows filled with richly-coloured glass, would be quite in place. Here in England the Perpendicular builders felt, and perhaps rightly, that our climate compels the architect to provide as much window as his skill allows.

CHRONOLOGICAL TABLE

General		Municipal and Ecclesiastical	Scholastic
B.C.	B.C.		
	c. 500.	Settlement of S. Catharine's Hill	
	c. 150.	S. Catharine's Hill settlement destroyed	
55. Julius Caesar's Expedition to Britain	c. 50.	Winchester first settled by Belgae	
A.D.			
43. Claudius' Expedition			
410. Romans leave Britain. "Rescript of Honorius"			
597. S. Augustine's Mission			
	662.	Minster begun at Winchester.	
	829.	Winchester becomes Capital of England	
	850.	Swithun, Bishop of Winchester	
	c. 860.	Winchester sacked by Danes	
871. ALFRED	c. 901.	Alfred buried at Winchester	
	903.	New Minster built	
	927.	Winchester besieged by Danes	
1066. NORMAN CONQUEST	1068.	William I crowned at Winchester in Old Minster	
WILLIAM I	1070.	Walkelin, Bishop	
1087—1100. WILLIAM II	1100.	William II buried at Winchester, in Walkelin's Cathedral	
1100—1135. HENRY I	1100.	Gifford, Bishop	
	1107.	Fall of Walkelin's Tower	

General	Municipal and Ecclesiastical	Scholastic
1135—1154. STEPHEN Civil Wars	1110. New Minster moved to Hyde Abbey 1115. Liber Wintoniae 1129. De Blois, Bishop	
1154—1189. HENRY II	1136. Foundation of S. Cross Rebuilding of Wolvesey 1141. Burning and destruction of city	
1189. RICHARD I Third Crusade	1172. Henry's son crowned in Cathedral 1174. Toclive, Bishop 1180. Hospital of S. Marie Magdalene 1189. De Lucy, Bishop 1194. Richard I re-crowned in Cathedral 1194. Rebuilding of East End of Cathedral	
1199. JOHN	1204. Peter des Roches, Bishop 1207. Visit of John. Birth of Henry at Winchester	
1215. Magna Carta 1216. HENRY III	1216. City in hands of Louis of France 1232-6. Castle Hall and Westgate built 1258. Parliament at Winchester 1265. Young Simon de Montfort takes city	
1272. EDWARD I	1276. Edward's first Parliament 1280. John of Pontoise, Bishop, founds S. Elizabeth College 1289. S. John's Hospital c. 1296. Stalls in Cathedral	

1307. EDWARD II	1324. Birth of Wykeham	
1327 EDWARD III	1345. Edington, Bishop. West End of Cathedral rebuilt	
1346. Crécy	1363. Wool Staple removed to Calais	
1348. Black Death	1367. Wykeham, Bishop	
1377. RICHARD II		1378. Papal Bull sanctioning College
		1378-86. Building of New College
		1382. Site for College purchased
		1387. Foundation stone laid
		1393 (? 4). Opening of College
1399. HENRY IV	1400. Wykeham's work in Cathedral begun	1400. STATUTES OF COLLEGE
	1404. Beaufort, Bishop	
1413. HENRY V	1420. Second Foundation of S. Cross by Beaufort	
1415. Agincourt		1426. Fromond's Chantry
1422. HENRY VI		1429-42. Waynfleete, Headmaster
	1447. Waynfleete, Bishop	1443. Foundation of Eton College with Waynfleete as Headmaster
		Visits of Henry VI
1454-71. Wars of the Roses		1474. Chapel Tower rebuilt
1461. EDWARD IV		

General	Municipal and Ecclesiastical	Scholastic
1483. EDWARD V. RICHARD III		
1485. HENRY VII	1493. Langton, Bishop. Hunton, Prior	
	1500. Fox, Bishop	
1509. HENRY VIII	1524. Silkstead, Prior	
	1528. Wolsey, Bishop	
	1531. Gardiner, Bishop	
1538. Suppression of Monasteries.	1539. S. Elizabeth College destroyed	
	1541. Monastery of S. Swithun passes to Dean and Chapter	
1547. EDWARD VI		
1553. MARY	1556. Mary married to Philip of Spain in Cathedral	
1558. ELIZABETH	1587. Charter of Queen Elizabeth	1570. Queen Elizabeth visits College
1588. Spanish Armada	1603. Royal visit.	
1603. JAMES I	Trial of Raleigh	
1625. CHARLES I	1632-5. Scrutiny of Laud	
Civil Wars		1639. Original Chapel panelling
	1642. City besieged by Waller	1640. Sick House built
	Battle of Cheriton	
	1644. City besieged and taken by Cromwell	
	Castle destroyed	

1649. Charles I beheaded	1648. Charles I at Winchester before his trial	1708. Lawsuit between Fellows and Warden
1649. PROTECTORATE	1659. Richard Cromwell retires to Hursley	1724. Dr. Burton, Headmaster
1660. CHARLES II	1661. Thomas Ken, Prebendary	1729. Warden Bigg
1666. Great Plague	1680-5. Charles II's Court at Winchester	1742. Old Commoners
	Royal palace built	1757. Warden Golding
1685. JAMES II	1685. Bloody Assize—Trial of Alice Lisle	1763. Warden Harry Lee
1687. Declaration of Indulgence		1766. Warton, Headmaster
1688. WILLIAM AND MARY		1778. Visit of George III
1702. ANNE		1789. Warden Huntingford
1714. GEORGE I	1713. Level of Choir raised in Cathedral	1793. Rebellion
1727. GEORGE II		1816. Goddard, Headmaster
1760. GEORGE III		1818. Brougham's Commission
		Last Rebellion
1820. GEORGE IV	1820-25. Extensive repairs in Cathedral	
	1827. New Bishop's Chair erected	

General	Municipal and Ecclesiastical	Scholastic
1830. WILLIAM IV		1832. Warden Barter
1837. VICTORIA		1836. Moberly, Headmaster
	1838. Corn Exchange built	
	1848. S. Cross Lawsuit, resulting in reorganisation	
	1853. New Cathedral Organ from Great Exhibition	1857. Public Schools Commission
		1861. Warden Godfrey Lee
		1866. Ridding, Headmaster
		1871. Old Governing Body superseded
	1873. New Guildhall opened	1874. New Statutes
	1876. County Hospital	
		1880. School Mission established
	1885. Repair of Cathedral Reredos begun	1884. Fearon, Headmaster
		1893. " Quincentenary "
1899. South African War		1901. Burge, Headmaster
1901. EDWARD VII		1902. S. African War Memorial
	1905-12. Underpinning of Cathedral	1904. First Warden under New Statutes.
1910. GEORGE V		1911. Rendall, Headmaster
1914-18. Great War		1922. War Memorial Cloister
	1930. " Friends of the Cathedral "	1924. Williams, Headmaster
		1932. Conversion of Brewery

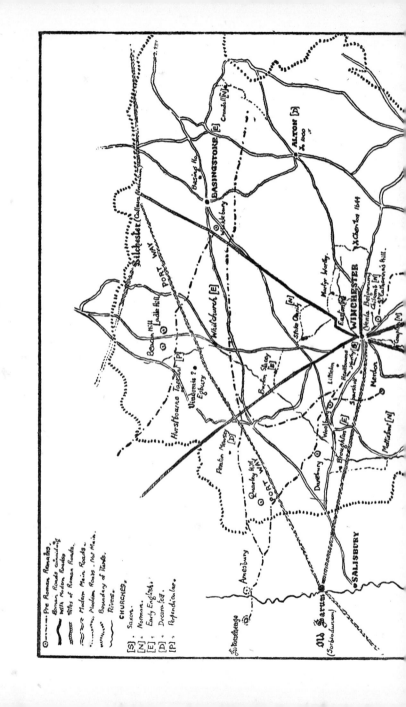

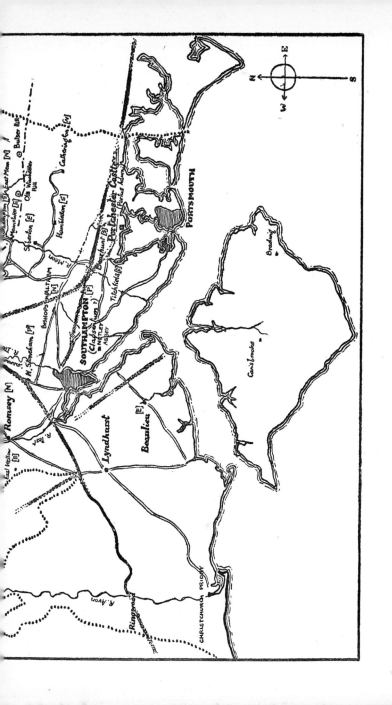

INDEX

D.K. McNaughton
Berwick a Tweed
November 1304 (6
replacement: